Special Effects Make-up

Janus Vinther

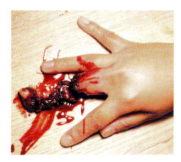

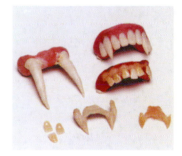

A Theatre Arts Book
Routledge
New York

A big thank you to all who have helped me by subjecting themselves to the various horrors and disfigurements depicted in this book.

A Theatre Arts Book
Published in the USA in 2003 by
Routledge
29 West 35th Street
New York, NY 10001
www.routledge-ny.com

Routledge is an imprint of the Taylor & Francis Group.

Cataloging-in-Publication Data is available from the Library of Congress.

ISBN 0-87830-178-X

Published in Great Britain in 2003 by
A & C Black Publishers Limited
37 Soho Square
London W1D 3QZ
www.acblack.com

ISBN 0-7136-6747-8

First published by Drama of Nygade 15, DK-6300, Graasten, Denmark

© Janus Vinther, 2002
English translation by Niels Coley

Photos by Janus Vinther (www.spfx.dk)

A & C Black uses paper produced with elemental chlorine-free pulp, harvested from managed sustainable forests.

Typeset in 10 on 13pt Myriad regular
Printed and bound in Singapore by Tien Wah Press (Pte.) Ltd

Contents

As far back as I can remember, I have been interested in the fantastic and the supernatural – preferably in the form of terrible monsters from the bowels of the earth or mystical beings from outer space. What started out as gory sketches in school notebooks, soon developed into experiments with masks and artificial wounds.

As a child, I once painted a polystyrene bust to make it look scary. I made a hole for the mouth and inserted a set of false teeth in the hole (I don't remember where they came from). I then hollowed out the back of the skull and mounted a red bulb in it. The result was a scary face that lit up in the dark, to the horror of my family. The seed was sown: I simply had to work with special effects for film and theatre. But it would be several years yet, and it wasn't until 1994 that I finally qualified as a make-up artist. Ever since then, friends and family alike have been forced to cope with gory effects and surprises when they least expect them.

I love working with special effects and the more dramatic they are, the better. But it's not as though my life revolves around gore and horror … I have a tranquil home full of plants! As a matter of fact, I find it difficult to watch real-life accidents or operations if they're shown on TV. However, special effects don't necessarily have to be horrific and gory; they can also be about creating fantasy beings, creatures from folklore, or simply making up a person to be as bald as a samurai. I've had many pleasant experiences working with film, theatre and events, and I hope that people's interest in special effects will continue to grow.

I am currently working as a teacher at a college called *EnJoy make-up*, and have a freelance private company, *SPFX* (www.spfx.dk), through which I create horror shows for children and young people, and also events for various firms.

I hope that this book will help to spread the knowledge of special effects and also improve their quality, so that we can create even better and more spectacular effects in the future.

Janus Vinther

Special effects help to make a film or play more visually spectacular. They are a manifestation of our imagination and, if done well, can provide us with mental images that may enrich our view of the world. But no matter how good special effects are, they can't on their own create a good film or play: this requires a good story and skilled actors. Special effects are merely a supplement to this, enhancing the visual experience.

Most people are highly visually perceptive and if special effects are poorly done, they will notice. However, special effects can be a number of different things. They can be effects involving backdrops, props, lighting, sound effects or computer graphics. This book only covers the kind of special effects that can be achieved with make-up, and the creation of artificial parts used in make-up.

When a film includes bloody special effects, a decision has to be made as to whether the effects are to be realistic representations, and how the audience will want them to look. There is quite a big difference. When a villain or a monster has its head blown to bits, it's often wildly exaggerated because it has to look spectacular. In reality, most bullet holes only leave a small hole in the skin. Conversely, real-life cuts and accidents sometimes look like special effects. I once showed some photos of real burns to some students and they thought it was a joke or examples of badly done make-up effects. Therefore, it is important to study reality to find out what cuts and accidents really look like. If you hurt yourself, it is a good idea to take pictures to document how it actually looked.

Finally, I would like to emphasise the importance of making sure that your special effects are suitable for your audience. Most people view special effects simply as entertainment and are amused when you demonstrate them for family and friends, or in public. But it's important to keep in mind that not everyone will find your special effects amusing and that they may be very frightening to small children!

Having written this introduction, I now bid you welcome to the exciting and fantastic world of special effects!

Special effects: a brief history

Special effects have been used since the early days of film. In 1895 the film *Demolition d'un Mur* (*Demolition of a Wall*) was shown for the first time in *Cafébio* (Paris). This film contains the first experiment in trick photography. The film was played backwards so the wall seemed to build itself up again. In the same year, the shocking historic drama *The Execution of Queen Mary* came out. In the film, she had her head chopped off and as trick photography was a new phenomenon, many people believed that an actor had sacrificed her life in the making of the film.

The use of special effects was soon taken a step further when in 1902 George Méliés made *A Trip to the Moon* and in 1904 *An Adventurous Automobile Trip*, both making use of clever special effects. Eighteen years later, in 1922, the world was introduced to the first actual horror film. In this film, *Nosferatu*, based on Bram Stocker's famous novel, *Dracula,* the vampire was represented as a bald-headed monster with two extra-long fangs. In 1922, Fritz Lang introduced the world to the first robot transformation on film in *Metropolis,* a political film about a future in which the poor are oppressed by a small ruling class and where the perfect woman, a robot woman, is created through a fantastic metamorphosis.

In the 1950s, sci-fi and horror films became immensely popular, especially films where human civilisation is threatened by titanic monsters destroying cities, or bizarre beings from outer space. These films paved the way for stop-motion technique, which allowed models of figures like King Kong and Godzilla to be animated as though possessing a life of their own. The special-effects creator Ray Harryhausen created effects for a number of films in the 1960s and early 1970s, animating figures from Greek mythology, dragons, skeletons and Cyclops.

In 1977, George Lucas created the film *Star Wars* and with the company *Industrial Light and Magic*, the world was introduced to new and exciting special effects, the likes of which had never been seen before. In the 1990s, computer-generated effects began to be used in film. Extensive use of these can be seen in films like *The Abyss, Terminator 2 (T2)* and *Jurassic Park*, in which fantastic scenarios were created with advanced computer graphics. However, computer-generated effects are unlikely to threaten the livelihood of special-effects make-up artists, as bullet holes can be imitated far more easily and more effectively with derma wax and artificial blood than with computer graphics. There is no doubt that in the future, monsters on film will be designed and visualised with powerful computers; computer graphics will replace previously used methods in the creation of monsters for the big screen. Having said that, there may in time come a reaction against large-scale, computer-generated special effects, so that the use of puppets, animatronics and actual-size models will have a revival.

This book deals merely with the small-scale effects which are not threatened by computer graphics – namely making up artificial wounds, the casting of small parts and torn-off limbs. Such effects are used increasingly in motion pictures, short-films, TV, photography, advertisements, theatre, shows, events, Halloween, role-playing games and other horror events. And, as the techniques and materials used in this book are within the reach of non-experts, I am able to present *Special Effects Make-up* as a handbook which allows the non-expert to create special effects in his or her home, using readily available materials and easily mastered techniques.

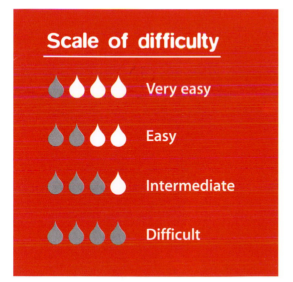

Scale of difficulty

Very easy

Easy

Intermediate

Difficult

1

Working with wax

Creating special effects with derma wax is very easy and more or less the ABC of artificial wounds make-up. In a short time, you can create effects which even at close range look both realistic and gory. Derma wax, which is a kind of 'skin wax', is used to simulate disfigurements of the skin. Originally used by morticians – for concealing injuries on corpses, to make the deceased look presentable at funerals – this wax comes in a range of different makes, each with their own unique colour and texture.

Here is a short guide to derma wax and similar products:

Grimas derma wax
A hard wax which requires a lot of pre-softening, for instance by mixing it with a rich moisturiser. It tends to be uneven in texture if not kneaded well enough before use. The wax is colourless and blends well with the natural colour of the skin.

Kryolan derma wax
A medium-hard, skin-coloured wax which is easy to soften – though it can be too soft.

Naturoplast
A medium-soft wax which retains its texture. Skin-coloured and easy to work with, it is sold in large cans only and is strongly perfumed.

Plastici
A medium-soft wax which is a bit sticky to work with. Skin-coloured.

Provax
A hard wax of a brownish skin colour, which requires a lot of softening.

Snazaroo wax
A medium-soft wax which tends to be of an uneven texture if not kneaded enough. The wax is of a strange yellowish colour and is easy to work with, though almost too soft.

Softputty
A very hard wax which requires a lot of pre-softening. It is very robust wax and can hold quite heavy objects. This wax is skin-coloured and not very sticky.

Steins derma wax
A very soft wax which, for some reason or other, is completely white. It doesn't stick to the skin very well, even though it is very soft; easy to model with, so good for modelling work.

Eyebrow wax
A hard wax which requires a lot of pre-softening. It tends to be uneven in texture if not kneaded well enough. This wax isn't dyed and blends well into the colour of the skin.

When creating a bloody wound, there are several things to consider. If the wrists are to be cut, it must be done along the artery; if done across the artery, the wound may not be opened up enough. Slash and stab wounds from a smooth-bladed knife (not jagged) usually leave a clean and regular cut in the skin – a jagged-edged knife, on the other hand, tears the skin more erratically. There may have been bacteria or poisonous substances on the knife, causing blood poisoning, swelling and discolouring of the skin.

Materials:
Derma wax, spatula, rich moisturiser, brushes, cream make-up (black, red, blue, brown, yellow), theatrical blood, fresh scratch or blood paste, porridge oats, desiccated coconut or tea leaves, Vaseline, talcum powder, turquoise-blue eye make-up, rubber tube and a disposable syringe (the kind with no needle).

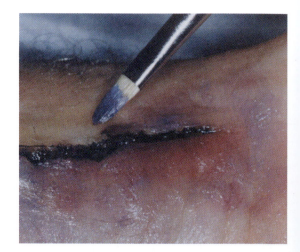

To model a broken eyebrow, put derma wax over the hairs of the eyebrow: this won't harm it and the wax can easily be removed again afterwards. Be careful not to let 'blood' run into the eyes, especially if the victim uses contact lenses, as it will stain the lenses red and theatrical blood is very difficult to remove from contact lenses.

To remove the derma wax, start by scraping it off with a spatula or spoon, or with tissue paper. Do not attempt to remove derma wax with a damp cloth, as it is water repellent and will be difficult to wash out of the cloth. When the actual wax has been removed, colour residue can be washed off with a wet, soapy cloth.

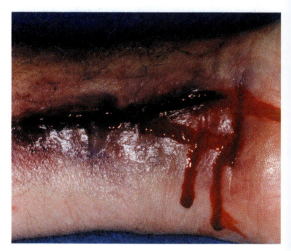

Roll a piece of derma wax into a cylinder the length of the wound. Press the wax onto the area of the wound, making sure that the wax cylinder isn't too high. Massage the edges with a little rich moisturiser, to make the transition to the skin less conspicuous. Scratch a gash into the wax with a spatula, but not all the way to ends of the cylinder. Jagged edges are quite easy to model using the spatula (see figs 1a and 1b).

Now paint the bottom of the wound black and the inside edge of the wound a dark red. Tint the outside edges of the wound reddish with bluish undertones, slowly blending the colour into the normal skin (see figs 2a and 2b).

If you want to model an older wound, close the opening of the wound slightly and use blood paste, fresh scratch, or a bit of crumbled porridge oats and desiccated coconut soaked in dark red and brown colour, instead of liquid blood. This will look like dried blood and scabs. An infected wound can be modelled using Vaseline with yellow make-up added to it.

Pour blood in the wound until you achieve the desired effect.

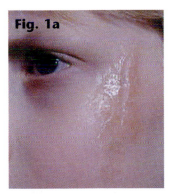

Fig. 1a

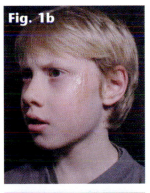

Fig. 1b

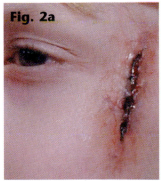

Fig. 2a

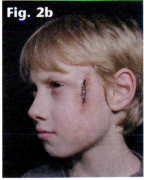

Fig. 2b

To model a wound with blood poisoning, paint turquoise-blue veins along the artery toward the wound with a thin brush.

If you want blood to gush out of the wound, you can use a very thin rubber tube. This has to be pretty strong, however, to stand up to the pressure of liquid flowing through it. Affix the rubber tube under the derma wax so that the opening is in the actual hollow of the wound. Attach a syringe containing theatrical blood to the other end of the tube. The tube may be difficult to conceal and for this reason it may be better in some cases to make a prosthesis, i.e. an artificial wound made out of latex.

Broken nose with no cut

Press some derma wax onto one side of the bridge of the nose. The idea is to make it look as if the nose is crooked or swollen. Make a smooth transition between wax and skin by smoothing out the wax at the edges. Tint around the swollen area with reddish and bluish shades – but avoid the swelling itself; this will make the swelling seem more prominent. Powder the swollen area with talcum powder (see fig. 1). Put theatrical

blood in one nostril and let it run a bit to look like a nose-bleed (see fig. 2).

If the accident happened some time ago, then make up the area around the nose with blue-red or brownish shades according to the rules on bruising (see page 52).

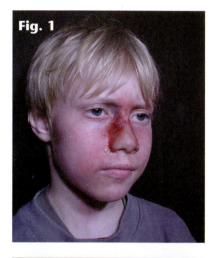

Fig. 1

Fig. 2

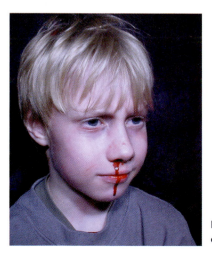

Nose-bleed
on its own.

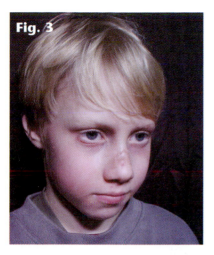

Fig. 3

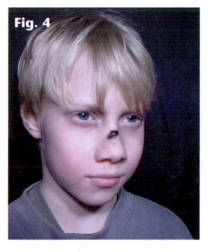

Fig. 4

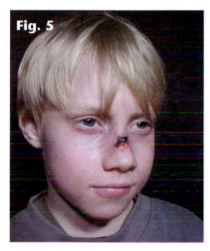

Fig. 5

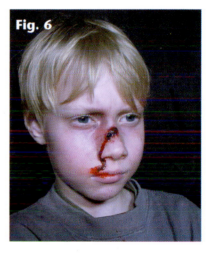

Fig. 6

Broken nose with a wound

Soften a very small piece of derma wax, roll it into a ball and press it onto the bridge of the nose, where you want the nose to be broken. The wax doesn't have to be put on completely straight. Press the wax flat and tone the transition from wax to skin to conceal the transition. Cut a gash in the wax with the sharp end of the spatula so it looks like the skin is broken. If you like, you can make the edges more jagged and open the gash slightly with the spatula (see fig. 3).

Now paint the base of the wound black and dark red. Close the wound slightly again so that the colour shows through the wax (see fig. 4). Tint the outer surface of the wax, and about 0.5 cm onto the skin with reddish and bluish tones. If you want bruising on the cheekbone under the eye, tone this area too (see fig. 5). Pour a little of theatrical blood into the wound and let it run down the nose. Be sure to let the blood run by itself (see fig. 6).

This effect can only be shown from above or slightly from the side, as the real finger is simply bent out of sight. If it is difficult to keep the finger in the right position, use sticky tape to keep it in place.

Materials:
Derma wax, rich moisturiser, a piece of plastic from a thin carrier bag, brushes, cream make-up (reddish-brown, red, blue, black, white), white Cernit, theatrical blood, toilet paper, spatula, liquid eyeliner brush.

The following are optional: 10 cm of rubber tube and a small ear-pump.

Soften a small piece of derma wax and roll it into a cylinder. Shape the cylinder into a ring around the joint of the finger, at the place where the rest of the finger is supposed to be torn off. Smooth the edge of the wax into the hand using a spatula and some rich moisturiser. It is important that there is sufficient wax to avoid getting a hollow between the ring and the finger joint: figure 1 shows the wrong effect; figure 2 the right one.

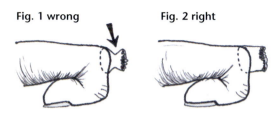

Fig. 1 wrong   Fig. 2 right

Make jagged edges on the inside of the ring to imitate shreds of skin. Place a small piece of plastic over the wax on the joint, then scratch the lines of the joint of the finger with the pointed end of a spatula or a wooden cosmetics spatula. The plastic prevents the lines from becoming jagged-edged, ensuring a more realistic look. Look at the other fingers to see how the lines look.

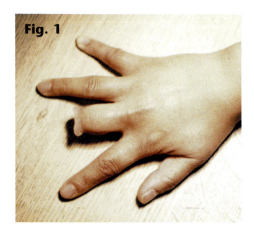

Fig. 1

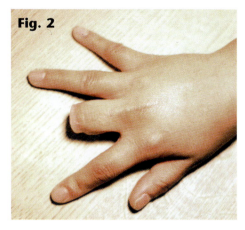

Fig. 2

Paint the lines a faint brownish-red colour with a liquid eyeliner brush (see fig. 3). Paint reddish and bluish tones towards the hand from the cut end of the finger, gradually blending these into the natural skin colour. Be careful not to overdo the colouring (see fig. 4).

In the middle of the ring, paint a small spot with white cream make-up. This is supposed to be the end of the bone. If you want it to look as if there's a bit of bone sticking out, press a bit of derma wax into the pit of the wound, and fix a small piece of bone-shaped

If you want the finger to look as if it has been squashed, a bit of toilet paper soaked in theatrical blood can be made to look like shreds of flesh, if put on the end of the remaining part of the finger (see fig. 7).

If you also want the cut-off part of the finger to be visible, you'll have to make a special cast of the finger. Place this in continuation

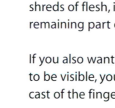

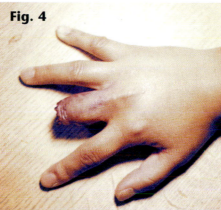
Fig. 3 **Fig. 4**

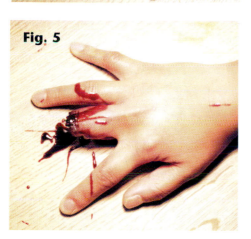
Fig. 5

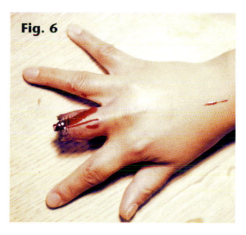
Fig. 6

white Cernit into it (you don't have to bake the Cernit). Paint the surrounding area on the inside of the wound black and dark-red. Pour a bit of theatrical blood into the wound (see figs 5 and 6).

of the finger, surrounded by loads of blood (see figs 8 and 9).

(See also the section on casting artificial body parts, on page 28).

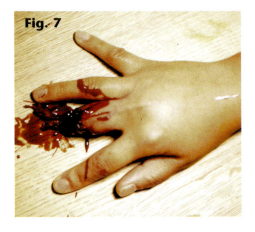

Fig. 7

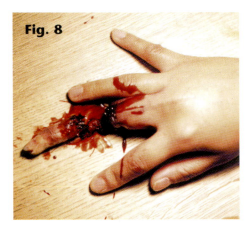

Fig. 8

Fig. 9

Squirting blood

If you want blood to squirt out, use a piece of thin rubber tubing. Most bicycle shops sell valve tubing by the yard (aquarium piping is too thick, and difficult to conceal). Affix the tube underneath the palm of the hand with the opening immediately beneath the derma wax ring. Mount the tube close to the skin underneath the hand and arm, making sure that the opening of the pipe isn't blocked by wax or cream make-up. Affix an ear syringe containing theatrical blood to the other end of the tube; most high-street chemists sell little ear syringes, well suited for this. If the derma wax isn't strong enough to keep the pipe in place, you can apply a little liquid latex with a brush. When the latex is dry and transparent, it should keep the tube in place.

Alternative finger made of wax

Instead of making up the finger and placing a latex finger in continuation of it, you can make the whole finger out of derma wax. This can be a bit difficult but, with the help of an artificial nail and a little painting, the illusion can be pretty convincing. Naturally, the real finger has to be bent out of sight.

Remember to powder the wax finger, to prevent it from looking shiny.

This effect is good for showing the finger being cut off with a knife. The wax is easy to cut, but in a film-shoot you should quickly cut to something else – the victim's cry of pain, for example – and then back to the finger. In the meantime, red shades have been added and a blood pump has been affixed underneath the finger, to create a more convincing effect.

For this you need a pack of artificial nails, but check the quality before you buy them – some artificial nails *look* far too artificial. An alternative method using gelatine is also described below.

Materials:
Derma wax, spatula, artificial nails, theatrical blood.

Press a small piece of derma wax onto the fingernail. Scrape a few lines in it with the spatula to make it look irregular and frayed. Dab a little theatrical blood onto the wax – already, it looks like a crushed finger (see fig. 1).

Press an artificial nail into the wax and skew it to make it look displaced (see figs 2a and 2b).

Alternatively, you can cut the artificial nail into several pieces and affix them to the finger as a splintered nail (see fig. 3).

If you simply want a squashed nail, put a thin layer of derma wax on the nail. Put a single drop of dark theatrical blood onto the wax, making sure that the blood only covers a small portion of the nail. Press the artificial nail into the wax in a normal position.

Fig. 1

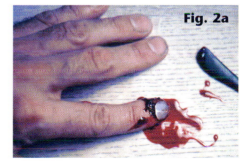

Fig. 2a

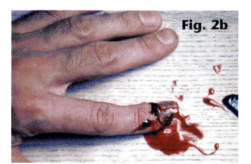

Fig. 2b

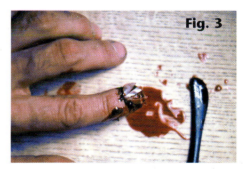

Fig. 3

Fig. 4a

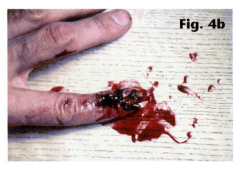
Fig. 4b

Idea: Make a cut along the finger towards the broken nail (see the section on bloody wounds, page 10). That will make it look like a pretty nasty accident (see figs 4a and 4b).

Squashed nail using gelatine

Cut a couple of nails out of a plate of gelatine. Cut 3–4 pieces for the same finger (see fig. 5). Pour boiling water into a small bow, then place a gelatine nail on the tip of the spatula and carefully dip it in the hot water until the gelatine goes soft. Be careful it doesn't fall into the water, as it will then dissolve (see fig. 6). The nail will now go soft

like a contact lens. Carefully mount the soft gelatine nail on the fingernail (see fig. 7). Repeat the process, so you get 3–4 gelatine nails on top of each other over the real fingernail. If necessary, smooth the surface with a little warm water on the spatula to remove irregularities (see fig. 8). Push a little theatrical blood under the gelatine to make it look like there is bleeding under the nail (see figs 9 and 10).

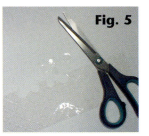
Fig. 5

Fig. 6

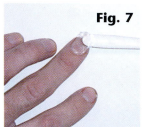
Fig. 7

Fig. 8

Fig. 9

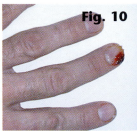
Fig. 10

The size of a bullet hole depends on a whether it's an entry or an exit hole. Where the bullet enters the skull or flesh it only leaves a small hole, and bits of clothing and skin may be drawn into the wound channel. When the bullet leaves the body again it takes with it flesh and blood and, in the case of a shot to the head, bits of skull and brain tissue. Other things to consider are the size of the bullet, its calibre, how powerful the weapon is and at how close a range the shot is fired. If it's for a film recording, agree which angle the shot is going to be viewed from and how much is going be visible.

Materials:

A small shirt button and a piece of thread, derma wax, rich moisturiser, mastix, cream make-up (black, red, blue), face powder or talc, theatrical blood, dark grey eye shadow, spatulas and brushes.

If the viewer is going to be able to see the actual impact of the bullet, small charges and pouches of blood will have to be concealed beneath the actor's costume. These 'blood bombs' are detonated by remote control, so that blood squirts out when the actor is shot. small metal plate under each charge protects the actor from the heat of the explosion.

Two ways of creating a bullet hole without using charges, are described in this section. It is important to note that these descriptions are merely a clinical description of a standard bullet hole: often, much greater damage is done to the skull than is described here, and bullet holes can look like severe skull fractures – or the whole back of the head may be blown away if a powerful firearm is used. The exit hole is far more 'open' than the entrance hole.

Procedure for entrance hole
Soften a small piece of derma wax and roll it into a ball. Press the wax ball onto the skin where you want the bullet hole to be (see fig. 1).

Massage and smooth the edges of the wax with a spatula to conceal the transition to the skin. Add a tiny bit of rich moisturiser to the wax to make it easy to model (see fig. 2). Now carefully make a hole in the wax with the pointed end of the spatula, being careful not to hurt the model. Press the wax with the hole flat, and fray the edges (see fig. 3).

Now paint the bottom of the hole with black cream make-up. Paint the inside of the wound and the low frayed edges dark red (see fig. 4). Tone with reddish and bluish shades from the surrounding area of the wound into the skin. If the wound looks too wet, you can powder it lightly with face powder or talc. Pour a bit of theatrical blood into the wound, but no more than is necessary, and allow one or two streams of blood to run out of the wound. You can also sprinkle a little dark grey eye-shadow powder or cigarette ash around the hole to look like gunpowder (see fig. 5).

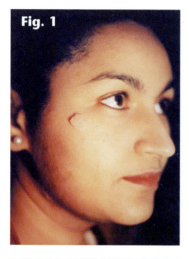

Fig. 1

Fig. 2

Fig. 3

Fig. 4

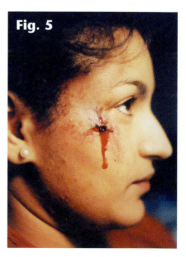

Fig. 5

Procedure for exit hole

Start by tying a piece of thread to a shirt button. Soften a small piece of derma wax and roll it into a cylinder. Shape it into a ring and place it round the shirt button, so the thread goes through the ring. Affix the whole thing to the 'victim' (see fig. 6).

The diameter of the shirt button should correspond to the supposed calibre of the gun. With mastix, make a circle of approximately the same size as the wax ring, where you want the bullet to exit the body. Press the button and wax onto the skin over the mastix and smooth the outer edges with

a spatula, using a little rich moisturiser. It's important to smooth the edges to completely conceal the transition from wax to skin (see fig. 7).

When the mastix is dry, and the wax ring with the button is glued in place, jerk the button out by pulling the thread. In this way, the wax is frayed from the inside as though a bullet had come out (see fig. 8).

Now paint the bottom of the hole with black cream make-up, and paint the inside of the frayed edges dark red (see fig. 9).

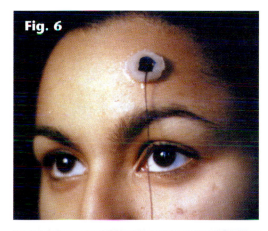

Fig. 6

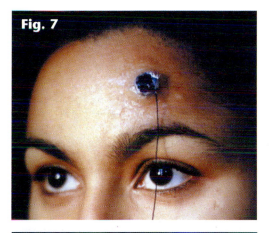

Fig. 7

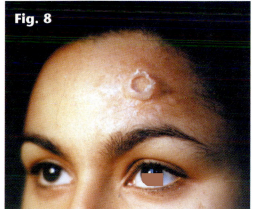

Fig. 8

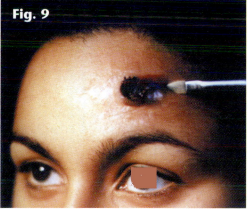

Fig. 9

Tone from around the frayed edges to the skin in reddish and bluish shades. Blend gradually into the colour of the skin (see fig.10).

If the wound looks too wet, powder slightly. Now pour theatrical blood into the wound – not too much – and let some of the blood run out of the wound onto the skin (see fig.11). It looks more realistic if the blood is allowed to flow naturally, so don't 'paint' the blood on with a brush.

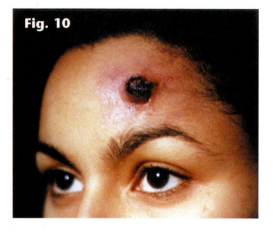

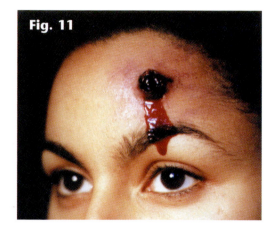

If you don't want the bullet holes to look fresh, use plenty of face powder or talc, making the wound look dry. Use blood paste or fresh scratch, which look more like dried blood, instead of theatrical blood. Give the person a pallid colour with a pale yellow make-up, to make it look as though the blood had left the body or coagulated in the veins. Also, make up the area around the eyes slightly darker, using grey-brown eye shadow, to make it seem as though the skin has fallen in slightly.

Products for modelling bullet holes.

When the murderer in a horror movie cuts his victim's throat, he does it from ear to ear. That way it looks as gory as possible.

Materials:
Skin tonic, derma wax, spatula, rich moisturiser, brushes, cream make-up (black, red, blue, yellow), face powder or talc, theatrical blood, latex, foundation or crème stick.

When using derma wax on the neck, you soon discover that the neck is quite soft, making it difficult to press the derma wax on. However, it can be done with a little ingenuity. Below are two different sets of instructions; one using wax, and the other using latex.

Procedure for wax
First, clean the neck with skin tonic. Soften a piece of derma wax and roll it into two cylinders, each approximately 6 cm long. Place them parallel on the victim's neck and smooth the edges with the spatula (see fig. 1).

Even though it may be difficult, it is important to conceal the transition to the skin as thoroughly as possible. Now fray the inner edges slightly. Roll two more cylinders, and repeat the procedure until you get the desired length for the cut.

Paint the bottom of the slit to make it look deeper, and colour the inside edge of the wound and the frayed part dark red (see fig. 2).

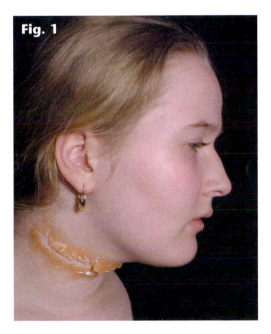

Fig. 1

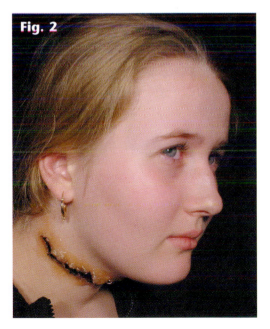

Fig. 2

From around the wound to the skin, tone lightly using dark red with a few bluish undertones. Be sure to blend gradually into the colour of the skin (see fig. 3). If the wound looks too greasy, powder it with face powder or talc.

Now pour theatrical blood into the cut. Allow several streams of blood to run down the neck (see fig. 4). Hold tissue paper underneath to keep blood from spilling on the victim's chest and clothes.

If you have difficulty getting the derma wax to stick properly, you can put a bit of latex over the wax and about 5 mm onto the skin.

If you want it to look like the victim has been bleeding for some time, tint the skin using a pale yellow cream make-up, foundation or crème stick. You can also put a bit of dried blood in the corner of the mouth.

If you want a really disturbing effect, splatter blood onto the victim's face and the floor or ground, so it looks like blood has spurted out during the cutting of the throat.

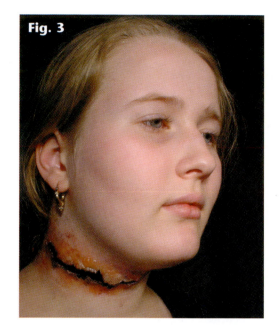

Fig. 3

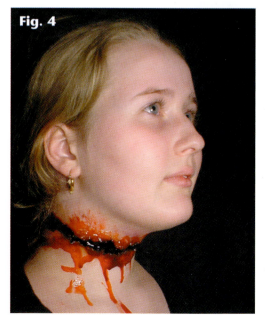

Fig. 4

Put a little extra blood on the floor for dramatic effect.

Procedure for latex

Materials:
Latex, face powder or talc, cream make-up (black, red, blue), theatrical blood, hairdryer, spatula, a piece of carrier-bag plastic.

The following are optional: 100–150 cm rubber tubing and a large syringe.

Place a small piece of carrier-bag plastic onto the neck where you want the cut to be. Apply latex to the neck in an oblong shape so that the plastic is covered and the latex goes a little outside the edges of the plastic all the way round. The latex should be about 1 cm thick over the plastic. Be careful not to get latex on your clothes. Dry the latex with a hairdryer; you'll know that it's dry when it becomes a yellow translucent colour. Repeat the process 4–5 times, then powder the neck lightly. Loosen the middle of the latex strip carefully and make a hole, being careful not to hurt the person's neck. If possible, carefully remove the plastic.

Enlarge the hole to a slit in the throat. Paint the actual slit with black cream make-up. Paint the inner edges dark red, and tone around the edges slightly with reddish and bluish shades. Blend from the latex onto the skin to conceal the transition. Pour plenty of theatrical blood into the wound.

If you want blood to squirt out, use a very thin rubber tube affixed underneath the latex and opening into one end of the slit. Affix the other end of the tube to a large syringe containing theatrical blood. Don't press it all out in one go, but in rhythmic pulses corresponding to the beat of the heart pumping out blood.

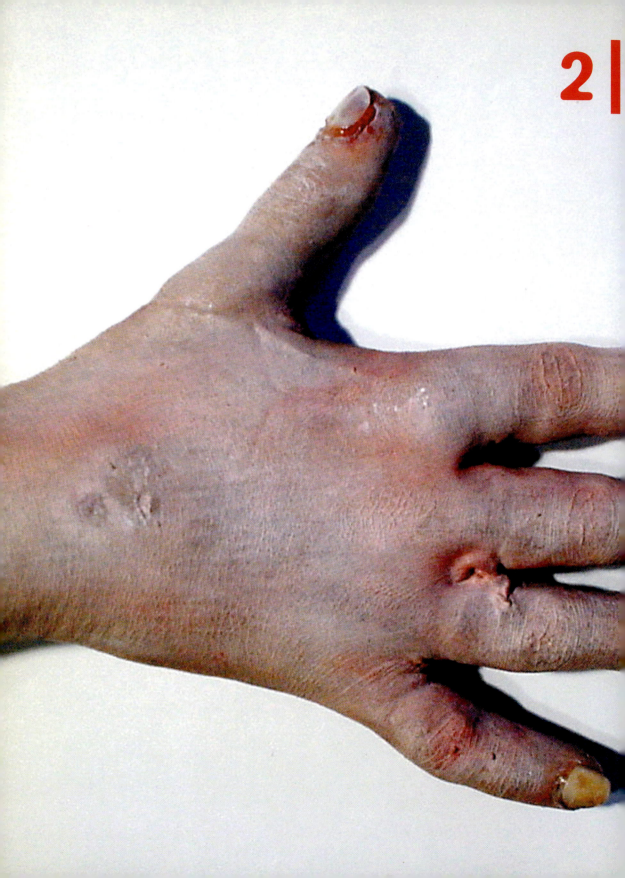

2

Artificial body parts

Depending on what it is you're going to make, artificial body parts can require a great deal of preparation. In some cases, you have to purchase special materials, but often you can manage with household items or hobby materials such as plaster of Paris and clay. Artificial eyes, for instance, can be made on a table top; while the casting of larger parts, such as an arm or leg, requires a larger, covered workspace. It's a good idea to wear work clothes and have special bowls and mixing sticks which are used only for making special effects.

Some of the artificial parts can be used in connection with special effects described elsewhere in this book. Effects like cut-off arms, legs and fingers can be used in conjunction with the 'torn-off and blown-off limbs' on page 82. Artificial intestines can be used with the 'opened gut' effect on page 90, and artificial bones can be used in connection with 'fractured bones' on page 98.

Most of the artificial parts are reusable props but may need to be refurbished after wear and tear. For instance, I had this chopped-off foot which I used for role-playing games and other events. In time, it became a bit tatty and soiled, so I gave it an extra lease of life with a new layer of latex, a little recolouring and fresh blood. If you use gelatine on reusable props you must remember to wash it off again – otherwise they will go mouldy after about three weeks.

⇨

A small prop, such as an artificial, bloody finger, can give rise to some quite amusing reactions!

Artificial arm

The mould for the artificial arm can be made directly from your own or a model's arm. If the arm is hairy, apply a thin layer of rich moisturiser or Vaseline to flatten the hairs. Do not use a model with very hairy arms: even if you put on plenty of moisturiser or Vaseline, long hairs will get in the way and it will hurt when you take the mould off, as the hairs will be stuck in the latex.

Pour some latex into a small bowl and paste the arm, hands and fingers with latex using your fingers, a spatula or a disposable brush. Keep the fingers spread apart during the whole process, which takes about 15–20 minutes. Be careful not to apply too much latex between the fingers as it can easily build up there, leaving a kind of 'inverted scar' between the fingers when the latex mould is removed.

When the whole arm is covered in latex, dry the latex with a hairdryer. You'll know that it is dry when it becomes translucent and a yellowish colour. Repeat the procedure about four times to get a thick enough layer of latex; it should be almost like a glove. When the final layer is dry, powder the whole arm thoroughly with talc – otherwise the whole thing will stick together when the latex glove is pulled off.

Loosen the edge of the latex from the arm and very carefully pull the latex glove off, turning it inside out while continuously powdering it with talc. On the outside of the glove there will be a perfect impression of the skin, which will make the arm look extremely realistic when stuffed. Powder the latex arm well, both on the inside and outside.

The pale, yellowish colour of the latex corresponds roughly to the skin colour of a person who has been dead for about a week. But if you want the arm to look like it's just been cut off, you have to add a little reddish shading to make it look 'alive'. There are two ways of colouring the arm: from the inside, or on the outside. The former method makes the arm look as it would after an accident, with discolouring and bruising, and the latter method gives a more even skin colour.

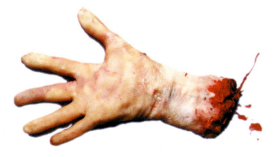

Colouring method 1

Pour a couple of drops of theatrical blood into the arm and rub it around to spread it to the desired areas, until you find the appearance of the limb satisfactory. If the blood doesn't spread properly, add a few drops of water. The idea is for the blood to be visible through the yellow latex skin.

Stuffing and bone

Stuff the arm with cotton wool. You may have to use plasticine cylinders for the fingers. Do this carefully and use the spatula if you choose to stuff the fingers with cotton wool. Don't over-stuff the fingers, as this will make them look swollen. Push small pieces of cotton wool carefully into the fingers, hand and finally the whole arm. Then place a few pieces of marine-blue cotton thread under the latex skin, to simulate the veins of the arm. Seen through the latex from the outside they will look like veins – but be careful not to overdo it. When the arm is sufficiently stuffed with cotton wool, seal the end with latex fluff. You can seal it off with bits of dried latex in the lid of and on the latex container, and whatever you may have spilled on the work surface: these bits of latex fluff, which look like little strips of meat

and sinews, can be stuck into the open end of the arm. To represent a piece of broken bone, use a bone made out of Cernit – or bones from your Sunday roast. If you use animal bones, these must first be boiled white to prevent them from going mouldy. Finally, pour liquid latex into the open end of the arm, to keep in the cotton wool and latex fluff, and dry the whole lot with a hairdryer. When the latex is completely dry, colour the strips of meat and the bloody end of the arm with dark red and black cream make-up and theatrical blood.

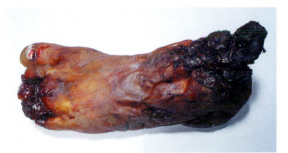

The foot is stuffed with cotton wool and the charred bone is a stick found in a forest.

Two fingers coloured to look gangrenous.

Colouring method 2

The stuffed arm can be coloured on the outside using foundation and a sponge. Be careful not to apply too thick a layer, as this will fill in the fine skin impression in the latex. After applying the foundation, colour the arm in brownish and reddish shades, creating your very own little work of art. Look at your own arm to see where there are shadows and reddish areas.

Putting on nails

Finally, you have to put artificial nails on the fingers (although the impression of the real nails may be so vivid that you don't need to do this at all). Cut the nails to the right shape and size and glue them on with mastix, nail-glue or latex. If you use latex or mastix, let it dry for about 15 minutes before pressing the parts together. Tone with a little red around the cuticles to get a realistic look.

Other parts

Artificial feet, legs, toes, hands and fingers are made in the same way. The procedure for ears and noses, however, is different – see the sections on casting these, on pages 38–44. A latex part typically lasts 4–5 years, after which it slowly deteriorates. Latex deteriorates faster when in contact with oil-based paints; for this reason, avoid oil-based paints if you want a long-lasting product.

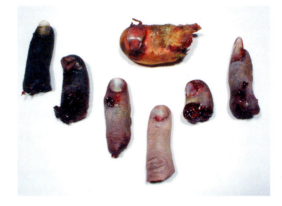

From now on, when you eat chicken or roast pork, keep the best bones and boil them afterwards! You can use them for special effects. Another possibility is to make artificial bones out of Cernit or Fimo clay.

Materials:

White Cernit or Fimo clay, an oven, a spatula, theatrical blood, yellow and brown water-based paints.

Cernit is available from hobby shops in small packets, and comes in all colours. It's rather hard coming straight from the packet and has to be softened by kneading it between your hands. It tends to crumble, but with a little patience, you'll succeed.

Roll Cernit into cylinders and shape them into bones – but these mustn't look like the kind of cartoon bones that Pluto eats! You can look in a book of anatomy or something similar to see what human bones look like. If the bone is for a broken arm or leg, the end of the bone which meets the body must be flat (see fig. 1). Mind that it doesn't end up looking like a slug; make sure the end is flat so it fits snugly against the arm. The other end is splintered: think of a broken branch and form splinters around the fractured area. If the bone has a clean fracture all the way through, the red marrow will be visible in the middle. Scratch lines along the length of the bone with a spatula.

Then place the finished bone in the oven on a piece of baking paper and bake for 15–20 minutes at 130°C / 250°F / gas mark 1. The temperature mustn't rise much above this, or the Cernit will then swell, become black and give off an unpleasant smell. If the Cernit stays in too long, even at the right temperature, it will slowly melt and turn a yellowish colour. After baking, cool the Cernit-bone at room temperature or in the fridge.

The bone is now ready to be tinted with yellow-brown, water-based colours, which will spread naturally in the grooved surface structure. If you want the bone to look old, paint it a dark yellow-brown colour with darker grooves. The marrow on the completely broken bone can be simulated with a little theatrical blood.

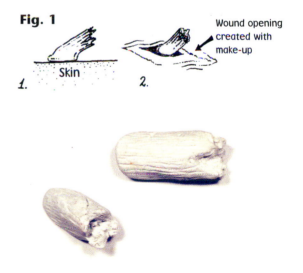

Fig. 1

Wound opening created with make-up

Skin

1.　　2.

Artificial bones can also be made out of other materials: for example doll clay, which forms a cracked surface when hardened, resembling the surface structure of bones. (Doll clay is a special kind of clay for the making of dolls.)

Artificial glass eyes or theatre eyes are either very costly, or look like something out of a cartoon. At a very low cost, you can make realistic, artificial eyes. Artificial eyes can be used for things like masks, the 'hanging-eyes' effect, Cyclops, monsters with gouged eyes and zombies.

Materials:

A polystyrene ball (about 2 cm in diameter) or a similar object the size of an eye – for instance the polystyrene dome shapes used to protect porcelain – a black marker pen, cream or water-based make-up in all colours, brushes, theatrical blood, ocean lacquer, water-based spray paint.

The following are optional: latex and an airbrush.

It's best if the polystyrene ball has a smooth surface; many of them have a rough one.

When painting an eye it is important to note the relative dimensions and what an eye really looks like. The actual eyeball is about 2.5 cm in diameter, although the visible almond-shaped part seems smaller. The pupil – the black disc – is actually a liquid-filled hollow and the front chamber of the lens, allowing light to pass through the vitreous body to the retina. The retina contains light-sensitive sensors, which react to different light waves. The iris surrounding the pupil has a pattern of lines radiating from the pupil to the outer edge. This is encompassed by a darker edge. The cornea covers the entire eye and gives the eye its jellyish appearance. When you look at an eye it reflects the light, for instance from a window, the sun, a lamp or a candle.

Note the relative dimensions.

Paint the pupil on the white polystyrene ball in the correct size, with a black marker pen or black water-based make-up or cream make-up. It is important that you get a regular edge around the pupil. Allow the colour to dry. Now paint the retina in the desired colours with an eyeliner brush or an airbrush. Add tiny radiating lines and patterns. Paint an edge around the entire retina with a darker colour and, on the eyeball, paint tiny, very fine veins with a little theatrical blood. Do not exaggerate and be sure to paint them wavy.

When you have finished and the paint is dry, apply the first layer of fixer lacquer. (If you use a liquid lacquer over the paintwork, it may smear the colours; and note that some types of spray lacquer contain solvents that dissolve polystyrene.) Now give the eye 3–4 layers of ocean lacquer, to give it that jellyfish surface. If you want a thicker jelly effect, you can coat the eye with liquid latex when the spray lacquer is dry, but before applying the liquid lacquer. Be careful not to put too much latex on, as it will give the eye an opaque appearance. However, this opaque effect can be used if you want to model an eye with a cataract.

You could also add an optic nerve. This can be made out of a piece of dried latex, rolled up and painted red with theatrical blood.

If you're going to affix the eye to a close-fitting mask, use half of a polystyrene ball to prevent the mask from bulging too much when worn.

Alternatives: Paint a pair of cat's eyes, snake eyes, vampire eyes or eyes with cataracts. When someone has a cataract, it looks like there's a whitish substance behind the retina.

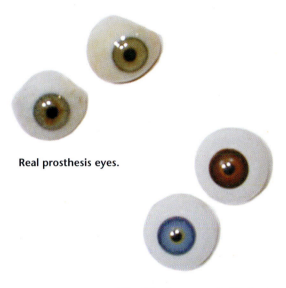

Real prosthesis eyes.

Theatrical eyes made of glass.

To make false teeth you must first make a mould. You can then cast and model the artificial teeth in Cernit or plastic, and the result will be a personal set of false teeth. The appearance of the teeth will depend on what they are going to be used for: you could make Vampire teeth, nerd teeth, troll teeth, pointed teeth, giant teeth or something entirely different. You can find plenty of inspiration in old horror films.

Tooth cast made with alginate

Materials:
Alginate, bowls, stirring stick, water, impression tray, clay, casting plaster or dental plaster (plaster which can be baked), cabinet file, brush, Shellac (optional).

Prepare the model to gape over a large impression tray of alginate. Pour about 1 dl. alginate powder in a bowl with about 1 dl. cold water. Stir until you get a yoghurt-like substance: you have to work quickly as the alginate dries in less than two minutes. Pour the alginate mixture into the impression tray (see fig. 1), and put the tray into the model's

Fig. 2a

mouth. Ask the model to bite carefully into the alginate. They must avoid biting all the way through the alginate, so that the teeth come into contact with the tray (see figs 2a and 2b). Wait for about 1 minute. The model will undoubtedly dribble a bit during the process, but that's OK.

Fig. 1

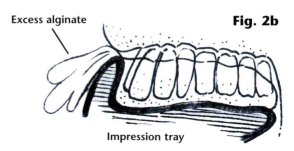

Excess alginate

Fig. 2b

Impression tray

When the alginate has changed colour and has hardened, loosen the tray carefully from the mouth. In the alginate you now have a perfect impression of the teeth. Don't leave the alginate too long before moving on to the next steps; it shrinks a little in contact with air, but if you keep the mould in a small bowl of water until the next materials are ready, it will be all right (see fig. 3). Build a wall of clay around the impression tray and the alginate mould. The wall should be about 3 cm high and encompass the whole tray, leaving no gaps (see fig. 4).

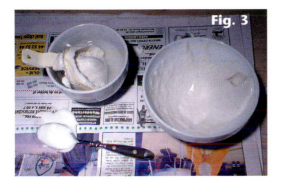
Fig. 3

Fig. 4

Pour about half a cup of plaster or dental plaster into a bowl and mix with the same amount of water until you get a substance like custard. Pour the plaster mixture into the area within the clay wall and fill right up to the edges. Tap the clay wall or the work surface lightly to create light vibrations that will bring small bubbles to the surface of the plaster. Tap lightly until no more bubbles come up, since these can cause deformities in the mould if left in the plaster.

Now leave the whole thing to dry for 2–4 hours. The plaster will become red hot after about 15–20 minutes because of the hardening process taking place. When the plaster goes cold again, leave it for at least 1–1.5 hours before separating the parts. Carefully wriggle the tray away from the hardened plaster and, lo and behold! You have a perfect imprint of the model's teeth. You can file the plastercast into a nice regular shape with a cabinet file, and carefully rinse the plaster to remove remaining bits of clay and alginate without harming it. You can also give the plastercast a coat of shellac to make it more durable (see fig. 5). Don't let bits of alginate and clay go down the drain as they will block it. Wash the moulds and your hands in a bucket of water, and pour the dirty water in the toilet when you've finished.

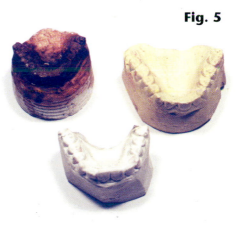
Fig. 5

Modelling teeth

> **_Materials:_**
>
> Plaster mould of teeth, Vaseline, gum-coloured and white mother-of-pearl-coloured Cernit or Fimo clay, spatula, aluminium foil, an oven.
>
> The following are optional: water-based make-up in various colours, Fimo lacquer.

First, apply Vaseline to the part of the plaster mould that the false teeth are to be modelled from. Then soften a piece of gum-coloured Cernit and build up the false gums around the plaster mould. Make sure that the mould is level and held securely in place. Only the front of the teeth will be visible, so it's most important that they look good from this angle. However, you also want a strong roof piece at the back, so that the teeth are securely seated in the mouth. Soften the mother-of-pearl-coloured Cernit and form the teeth, which are then embedded in the false gums (see fig. 6). Make sure that the teeth are securely rooted in the gums or they will fall out when you start to use them. Scrape a structured surface onto the teeth and gums, using a spatula.

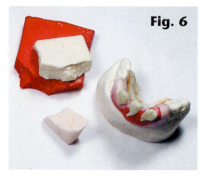

Fig. 6

When the model is finished, put it in the oven on aluminium foil. Bake it for about 15–20 minutes on 130°C / 250°F / gas mark 1, depending on the size of the teeth. If the temperature rises too much above this, the Cernit will swell, go black and give off a bad smell. If you leave the Cernit in the oven for too long, even on the right temperature, it will slowly melt and turn a yellowish colour.

After baking, cool the teeth at room temperature or in a fridge. Loosen the false teeth very carefully from the mould by wedging a spatula between the mould and the model. The Cernit cracks easily so it's best to ease it off from several angles at the same time. Now you can paint the false teeth with water-based make-up colours, for instance if you want the teeth very yellow and bloody. You can also apply a coat of Fimo lacquer.

The finished teeth fit easily into the mouth, but are not particularly strong and may break if not handled with care.

Throw left-over bits of plaster and alginate in the bin – not in the sink, as they easily block the drain.

Acrylic teeth

Materials:
Plaster mould of teeth, cold-cure acrylic set, separation fluid (this usually comes with the cold-cure acrylic set), a spatula or wooden cosmetics spatula, disposable brush.

This method requires good ventilation, as the cold-cure acrylic gives off very strong fumes which can be hazardous to your health if breathed in for any length of time. A dust mask is also recommended. Pregnant women must not work with cold-cure acrylic or inhale fumes from it, as it can cause damage to the foetus.

With a brush, apply a layer of separation fluid to the plaster mould. Coat the teeth to be modelled, the gums and across the roof of the mouth, applying 4–5 layers and leaving to dry between each layer. Paint evenly, and make sure you get into all the little nooks and crannies.

The material cold-cure acrylic consists of three components: white tooth powder, pink gum powder and a translucent acrylic fluid. Put about 1 teaspoon of liquid into a small glass or metal container about the size of the lid of a 1.5 litre pop bottle. Put the same amount of white powder in a container the same size. Now you'll need a wooden cosmetics spatula, a pointed spatula or a small disposable brush.

First, dip the utensil into the fluid, then into the powder so that you get a small blob of glaze. Apply the glaze to the plaster mould, thereby building up the teeth. Continue applying glaze until you have built up the desired teeth. Use the gum-coloured powder for the gums and the roof of the mouth, which will hold the whole thing together. This is a slow process, but you have to work without breaks, as the glaze hardens quickly and cannot be softened again after hardening.

When the modelling is done, leave the teeth to dry for a while. However, before they harden completely, they must be removed very carefully from the plaster mould. Wedge a spatula between the model and the mould and carefully ease it loose. Then leave to dry completely. Do not put the teeth in your mouth until they are completely dry, after about 4–5 hours. You can file the false teeth carefully with a nail file if they have uncomfortable irregularities. Acrylic teeth are very robust and the colours closely resemble those of real teeth and gums. A set of acrylic false teeth is made out of the same material as real false teeth and completely non-toxic once hardened.

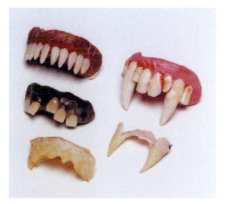

Shape and paint your false teeth any way you want them.

Below are instructions for making moulds to cast latex parts. Latex parts can be worn on the face or body, or mounted on a mask.

These parts are modelled in plasticine. Ordinary clay cannot be used; the reason for this is that you have to make negative plaster moulds, and when the moulds harden, the plaster gets very hot. This will dry the clay out and make it difficult to remove from the mould without breaking it.

Casting plaster is preferable to ordinary modelling plaster. Modelling plaster isn't robust enough and won't last for as many casts; casting plaster, on the other hand, is rock-hard and can be baked. Use fine-grained casting plaster of the same kind as dentists use for the casting of teeth.

Procedure for making horns

Materials:
Plasticine, spatula, knives, modelling utensils, bristle-sponge, casting plaster, plastic cup, water, latex, hairdryer, face powder or talcum powder.

Study a pair of real goat's horns to get an idea of the surface structure and shape. You don't have to attempt to copy them exactly, just get an idea of how the real thing looks.

Shape a pair of horns in plasticine - straight, twisted or curved, depending on the figure they are to be mounted on. It is important that you make the end piece flat so it can be attached and glued to a head or a bald cap. Scratch grooves on the surface of the horns with a knife or a flat spatula, to give them a realistic structure. If you want the horns to have a perforated surface structure, make impressions on the surface with a bristle sponge.

Mix some casting plaster in a disposable plastic cup, or in some other container that is slightly bigger than the horn you are going to make. Alternatively, you can make a container out of clay. Gradually add water to the plaster powder while stirring continuously. The plaster is ready when it has a consistency like custard. Do not fill the cup or container completely with plaster, but leave a little space at the top (about 15%).

Powdering.

Affixing hair.

Carefully insert the horn, pointed end first, into the cup or container until the whole horn is submerged and only the clay end-piece is visible. You can put a large screw in the plasticine horn to make it easier to remove it from the mould again.

Now leave the plaster to dry for 2–3 hours. After 15–20 minutes the plaster becomes very hot and then cools again slowly. When the plaster mould has cooled down, leave it to dry for another couple of hours and then remove the plasticine horn, which will be ruined in the process. You can simply roll the plasticine up and use it again.

Mould for horn in a container made out of clay.

The same procedure is used for constructing artificial noses, artificial chins or any other modelled excrescence you wish to mould.

Rinse the plaster mould under warm water to remove any remaining plasticine, and your mould is ready to make a latex cast. Pour latex into the mould, filling it completely. Then pour the latex back into the bottle or bowl, so that you are left with a thin layer of latex remaining on the inside of the mould. Leave the latex to dry at room temperature – or dry it with a hairdryer, but don't hold the hairdryer too close to the mould as the hot

Stuffing with cotton wool.

Colouring.

air is thrown back and may cause the hairdryer to overheat. Now pour a new lot of latex into the mould, making sure it gets distributed evenly, and pour it back as described above. Repeat the process of drying and applying a new layer of latex 4–6 times, until you have a thick enough layer. When the final layer is completely dry, use a brush to powder the latex in the mould with face powder or talcum powder. Then grip a corner of the latex and pull it out of the mould. The horn can now be coloured and mounted. You can colour the horn with cream, water-based or rubber make-up.

When making an artificial nose you need a model to work from. You can use a glass bust or a cast of a face.

The quick method

Here is another method for making horns, which has the advantage of being quicker than the one described above, as you don't have to make a plaster mould. However, the result won't be quite as detailed.

Shape a horn, a nose or something entirely different out of plasticine. You don't have to pay so much attention to detail as only the coarser features will be apparent in the end result. Apply liquid latex directly onto the clay mould for this method. Dry thoroughly with a hairdryer between each layer of latex. It's best to blow-dry with cold air, otherwise the plasticine may melt under the heat of the hairdryer.

After 4–6 layers of latex have been applied, and the final layer is completely dry, powder with talc or face powder. After carefully removing the horn, it is ready for use. Note that if you leave a latex cast on a plasticine mould for several days, a reaction takes place between the plasticine and the latex, so that the latex swells in patches and becomes deformed. Therefore, always finish a project and remove the latex part on the same day or the following day. If you have modelled a fine surface structure on the clay after all, you can turn the horn inside out to make the structure more clearly visible – but laterally reversed. The horn is now ready to be coloured and mounted. If the product is a nose, you can't turn it inside-out, as it won't look right.

Mounting

Affix the artificial latex parts with mastix, prostick or more latex. Before mounting latex parts on skin, make sure you cleanse the skin with skin tonic. Apply glue to the surface and let it dry for 1 minute for the stickiness to develop. Then press the latex part in place and hold until the glue is dry. If you have difficulty getting the latex part to stick, then apply a little latex around the edges and dry with a hairdryer.

When blending in the latex part with colouring, it may be difficult to get a smooth transition from latex to skin: the latex part absorbs colour differently from the skin, making the colours look stronger on the latex part. To make a smoother transition, apply a little flexible sealer-lacquer with a brush. Note that sealer-lacquer takes a long time to dry.

Removal

Smaller latex parts are removed in the same way that you remove a plaster. With larger parts you have to be more careful, to prevent damage to the person or model, but also to the latex part, if this is to be re-used. If you have used mastix glue, this can be dissolved using mastix remover – but use this very sparingly, applied to a cotton bud, as mastix remover is a solvent and may irritate the skin.

When creating artificial ears and earlobes, you first have to make a plaster mould from a real ear. Then you model the ear from the plaster mould. Here are some suggestions for things to make: Elf ears, Mr Spock ears, troll ears, pierced ears or elephant ears – the only limiting factor is your own imagination. If modelling a cut-off ear, skip the plasticine phase, and do the latex work directly on the plaster mould.

Materials:

Plastic carrier bags, scissors, ordinary clay, alginate, cotton wool, bowls, spoon, face powder or talc, casting plaster, plasticine, acetone, latex, spatula, hairdryer, cream make-up, water-based make-up and theatrical blood (optional).

Fig. 1

Making the plaster mould

Have the person you are modelling from lie down comfortably with their head to one side. With a pair of scissors, cut a small hole in a piece of plastic bag and stick the ear through the hole, so that only the ear is visible. Put a small piece of cotton wool into the earhole, but only enough for the cotton wool to just cover the entrance. Build up a 4–5 cm high wall of clay around the ear and make sure that it holds tight where it meets the head (see fig.1).

Fig. 2

Mix alginate and cold water in a bowl, about a cupful of each; you have to work quickly, as alginate hardens in less than a minute. When the mixture has an even texture like yoghurt, pour it into the clay-mould, up to a level of about 1–2 cm above the ear. There mustn't be lumps in the alginate: if there are, it isn't mixed well enough. The alginate is dry when it changes colour (see fig. 2).

Carefully ease the clay mould and the alginate away from the ear and place it down carefully with the earhole facing upwards. Remove any bits of cotton wool from the earhole area of the alginate mould. Moisten the alginate with water; alginate shrinks a little in contact with air. Fold clay around the negative alginate mould of the ear to make the wall higher (see fig. 3), making sure that the clay wall is completely tight, as liquid plaster easily finds its way through the clay and breaks the 'dam'.

Fig. 3

In the meantime, mix a small bowl of casting plaster, gradually adding water to the plaster while stirring continuously. The plaster is ready when it has the same consistency as custard. Pour the plaster into the mould, right up to the edge (see fig. 4). If the clay wall seems unstable, you can put your hands around it for support until the plaster starts to harden, to prevent the mould from leaking. While the plaster is hardening, it gets warm; when it has gone completely cold again, very carefully take the mould apart. Remove the clay and alginate, and clean the plaster with a small spatula or stick. If the clay isn't yet dry, you can roll it into a ball and re-use it. Clay must be wrapped up securely to prevent it from drying out.

Fig. 4

Modelling ears

When the plaster model is ready, the ear can be modelled in plasticine. This can quite easily be shaped on the plaster mould using a spatula or your fingers. Sharp edges between the plasticine and plaster can be made by dabbing a little acetone onto a spatula and running it lightly along the edge. Acetone dissolves plasticine (see fig. 5).

Fig. 5

Throw leftover bits of plaster and alginate in the bin – not the sink, as they will block the drain.

Making a latex ear

When the ear is finished, apply latex with a brush – or dip the ear into a bowl of latex. Never use quality brushes, as you can't get dry latex out of the hairs; use a spatula or your fingers instead (see fig. 6). When the ear-mould is covered in latex, leave it to dry or use a hairdryer for a quicker drying time. A latex ear requires 3–5 layers of latex before it can be removed from the plaster model.

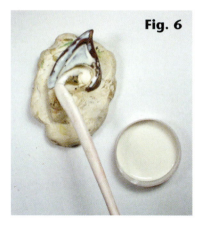

Fig. 6

Latex is dry when it becomes yellowish and translucent: if there are white specks in it, it isn't dry. When the latex is completely dry, the ear is ready for colouring with cream, water-based or rubber make-up. This can be done using an ordinary brush or a sponge. Optionally, you can apply a final layer of latex after colouring to seal the colour. Then powder the entire ear with face powder or talc. If you don't powder the latex ear, it will stick together when you remove it from the plaster mould. Grip a loose flap and very carefully pull the ear out of the form. Then cut off any loose shreds with a pair of scissors. If the plaster model breaks, it can be glued together again using superglue or nail-glue. Use mastix-glue to fix artificial ears, or parts of ears, to a model or to a person's ear.

To make a bloody, torn-off ear, stuff the earlobe with cotton wool and put a bit of latex fluff with bits of dried latex onto the torn-off area. Mix the left-over bits of latex with a bit of liquid latex to seal the cotton wool and latex fluff. Dry with a hairdryer and apply a little theatrical blood, to make it look like flesh, sinews and shreds of skin. Leave to dry again (see fig. 7).

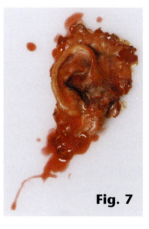

Fig. 7

You can also fix bits of latex 'skin' onto the ear, to make it look as though it's been torn off.

When you see entrails on film, they are usually real animal entrails, which can be bought at the butcher's. But if you cannot get hold of the specific entrails you need, or if there are other problems, it's nice to know how easily these things can actually be made.

Materials:

Cotton wool, latex, spatula, hairdryer, theatrical blood, cream make-up in all colours, lacquer, rich moisturiser.

When creating artificial entrails, you need a little knowledge of how the real thing actually looks. Get hold of a medical book with colour photos. These can be bought in specialist bookshops or borrowed from the libraries of universities, medical schools or hospitals. Here is a book with plenty of colourful photographs:

Colour Atlas of Anatomical Pathology, by Robin A. Cooke & Brian Steward (1995)

Below, the procedure for making a liver is described.

Make a careful study of the size and colour of the entrails you want to model. Take a piece of cotton wool of an appropriate size and soak it in latex; you can then shape it quite easily with your fingers or a spatula. Dry the entrails with a hairdryer at regular intervals to maintain the shapes that you have formed (see fig.1).

If you're not satisfied with a part of the entrails, put a thin piece of cotton wool over it and apply liquid latex until you get the desired result (see fig. 2). Keep turning the

Fig. 1

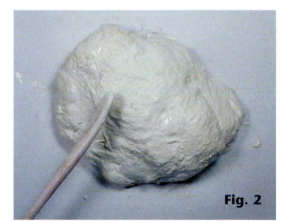

Fig. 2

cotton wool over, working on both sides since the cotton wool will go flat on one side if allowed to dry on a flat surface.

When you have finished shaping the entrails, leave them to dry thoroughly. Colour the product with make-up and theatrical blood. Finally apply a layer of lacquer to give a shiny surface.

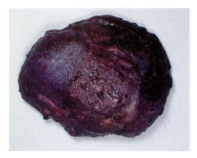
Coloured.

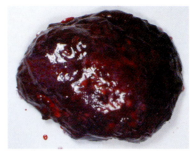
Lacquered.

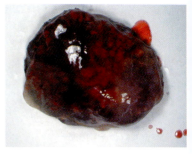
With slime.

When you use the entrails, apply moisturiser, cleansing lotion or something else slimy to look like tissue fat. To make long, thin sinews or veins, pour a little latex onto a wooden tabletop or glass plate. Leave it to dry and then roll it up in strips so you get elastic threads. These latex sinews can now be attached to the entrails.

If it's a heart you are making, you can insert a plastic tube into it to represent the aorta. Attach an ear syringe to the other end. When you pump, it will look as though the heart is still beating after being torn out.

Materials other than latex can also be used: here is a stomach ulcer made from insulating foam (for insulating windows), which has then been coloured.

When the latex has dried thoroughly, you can paint it with cream or rubber make-up, and mix in some theatrical blood to get a bloodier colour.

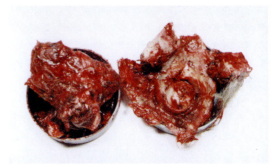

When working with special effects, you often have leftover bits of bloody latex or derma wax. Keep them in a container and use them for other effects at a later date.

You can make an artificial hand with claws and warts as a glove, which you can easily get on and off. Simply model the hand onto a pair of cloth or surgical gloves. You can also make a latex glove as explained on page 28. It's important that the glove can be easily put on and taken off, so it doesn't break the first time it is used.

Materials:

Latex, cotton wool, a pair of cheap cloth or surgical gloves, a glass bowl, spatula, hairdryer, artificial nails, water-based or cream make-up in selected colours.

The following materials are optional: face powder or talc, artificial hair and theatrical blood.

Put on one of the gloves. Dip small pieces of cotton wool in latex and put them onto the glove. Shape and smooth the latex-soaked cotton wool into the desired shape (see the photo series overleaf). Add more cotton wool and latex, thereby gradually building up the monster hand. Note how smooth and even a surface you can get when smoothing with a spatula. When the back of the hand is finished, dry it with a hairdryer. Model the palm of the hand in the same way.

When the modelling is finished, it's best to take off the glove before colouring and affixing additional details. Lift up the edge of the glove slightly and pour in some face powder or talc to make it easier to remove (see fig. 1). If you are using a surgical glove, it may be a little awkward to get it off, as the glove is tight-fitting and the latex less elastic than the glove itself. Be careful not to break

the glove when you pull it off. Lightly pull the fingers of the glove and straighten them again when you've taken the glove off. If you find that you have made a hole in the gloves, this can easily be repaired using a little cotton wool dipped in latex.

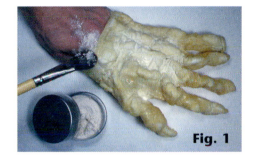
Fig. 1

Now dab a little latex onto the fingertips and affix the artificial nails. To ensure that the nails stay in place, put a drop of latex on the topside of the fingertips, at the root of the nail. You can also shape the latex to resemble cuticles. Finally, dry both the latex and the nails.

Now the hand is ready to colour with water-based or cream make-up. If the hand is very stiff, you can use water-based make-up colour, which is the easiest to work with. On the other hand, if the hand is very flexible and thin, cream make-up is recommended as it is more pliable and won't flake off as easily as water-based make-up. If working with cream make-up, powder well afterwards to prevent colour from rubbing off.

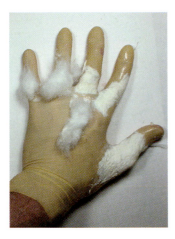
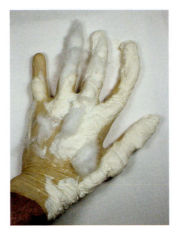
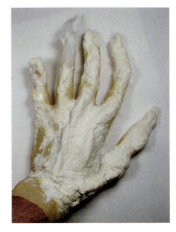
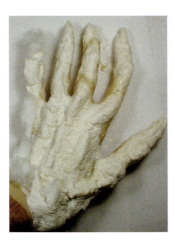
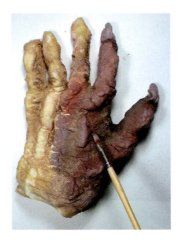
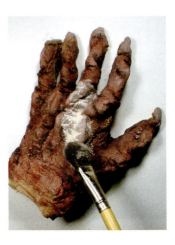
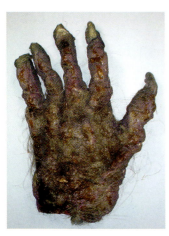

Artificial hair can be glued onto the hand using latex: simply dip one end of a lock of hair in liquid latex and fix it to the hand where hair would normally grow. A nice detail is to put lighter hair on as a first layer – let the latex dry – and then put darker hair on top. This will make it look more natural. If it is a very hairy monster, you could let fur come down the hand slightly from the wrist, but don't overdo it.

You can also model bloody wounds on the hands as well as warts, abscesses, lines and scars. Only your imagination sets the limits: see the dragon claw below.

Advice on the use of gloves
If the gloves are sufficiently thin and not too stiff, it may be a good idea to turn them inside out after use; after a play, for instance, there will be sweat and condensation in the gloves and this won't be able to evaporate. (Naturally, this cannot be recommended if the gloves are very detailed, or have ornamental features on the outside which are fragile and may break when the glove is turned inside out.) In any case, always air the gloves near an open window.

Remember to shape and colour the palm of the hand too. The palm is often lighter than the back of the hand.

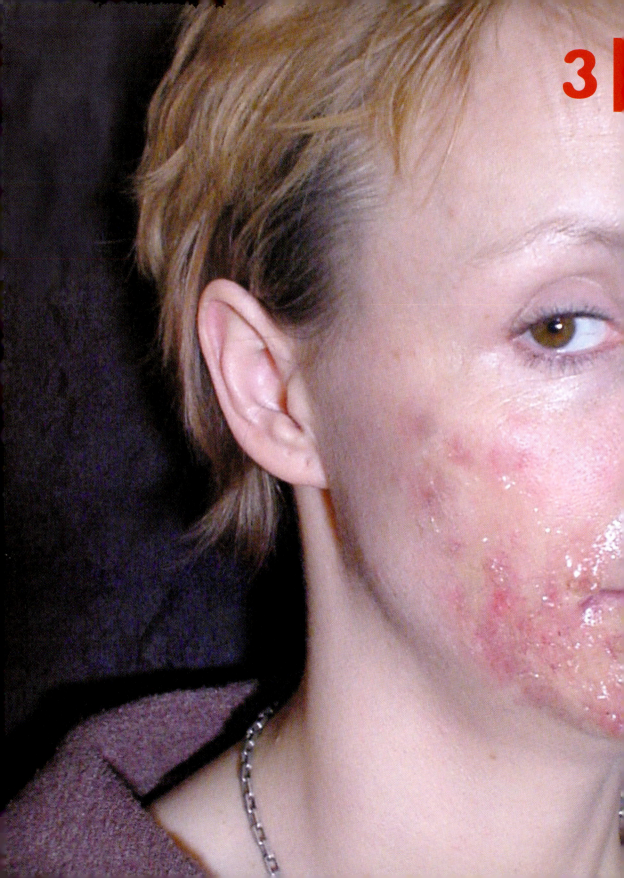

3

Other effects

This chapter covers a number of special effects at different levels of difficulty. Bruises, grazes and skin ailments are pretty straightforward to do, while effects such as ageing require a little more practice.

The ageing effect is best suited for events such as theatre and parties, where it will be viewed from a distance of at least a couple of metres. The reason for this is that the described ageing techniques may look too 'made-up' when viewed close up. Making up someone to look old at close hand, requires a knowledge of latex foam mask production, which isn't covered in this book.

Furthermore, this chapter covers the making of artificial blood, brains, vomit and other 'unmentionable' substances for use in film and theatre. These unpleasant substances, which can all be made from household materials, are often used in scary films and for dramatic events.

Bruises are caused by an impact, as a result of which the tiny veinlets, or capillaries, beneath the skin are haemorrhaged, causing minor internal bleeding. Through the skin, the bleeding appears as bruising in different colours. Bruises are generally categorised into five stages ranging from the moment of bruising until the bruise finally heals and disappears again a number of days later.

Bruises

Materials:
Cream make-up or eye shadow (dark red, blue, green, yellow), sponge, brush.

Bruises are done either with cream make-up or with eye shadow. Choose your colouring according to the stages listed below. Blend the edges of the make-up well into the skin to get a more realistic look, using a sponge, a brush or your fingers. Go for an irregular and asymmetrical shape (see figs 1a and 1b). This toning and colouring technique can also be used for most special effects injuries where the surrounding skin is discoloured.

The five stages of bruising:
1. The skin is a reddish colour.
2. The skin turns a bluish red or dark violet.
3. The skin becomes a more brownish colour.
4. The colour changes to a yellowy green.
5. The bruise remains yellow until it is healed, and no longer visible.

Fig. 1a

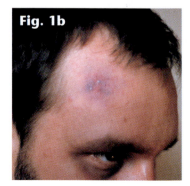
Fig. 1b

Simple grazes

Materials:

Cream make-up (dark red, brown), sponge, brush, bristle-sponge, theatrical blood, soil or dirt.

Tone the skin very lightly with dark-red cream make-up. Apply a little theatrical blood or dark-red and brown cream make-up to a bristle-sponge, then dab the graze lightly with the sponge, to simulate small specks of blood (see fig. 2). If the graze is supposed to be caused by a fall, draw the sponge very lightly across the grazed area so you get little lines. You can also sprinkle a bit of soil or dirt into the graze (see fig. 3).

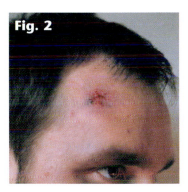

Fig. 2

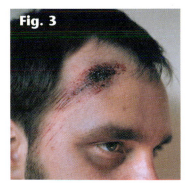

Fig. 3

Deeper grazes

Materials:

Derma wax, rich moisturiser, spatula, black bristle-sponge, cream make-up (dark red, blue, brown), theatrical blood, soil or dirt.

Soften a piece of derma wax the size of a large pea, and press it onto the desired area. Blend the edges into the skin with a spatula, so that the transition is no longer visible. Add a little rich moisturiser to the wax to make it easier to spread. Press the bristle-sponge hard against the derma wax and remove it again carefully. Now the surface structure of the sponge is imprinted into the wax, so it looks like grazed and damaged skin.

Tone the wax graze with reddish, bluish and brown cream make-up colours. Sprinkle a little theatrical blood onto it or dab with blood on a bristle-sponge. Press a little soil or dirt into the graze, but don't overdo it. Let a little blood run from the graze (see fig. 4).

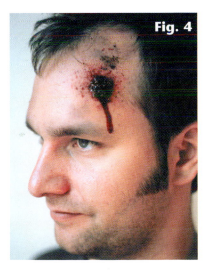

Fig. 4

A fake tattoo can be used for films, events, parties and photoshoots. Typical tattoo subjects are Celtic patterns, graphic patterns, Chinese lettering, dragons, women and skulls. You can find plenty of inspiration in tattoo magazines. Choose the desired subject and consider whether it suits the place you have chosen – e.g. the neck, shoulder, back, stomach, ankle or upper-arm.

Freehand with a ballpoint pen

Materials:
Rough sketch of an idea for the tattoo, dark-blue ballpoint pen, marker pen, talcum powder.

A temporary tattoo can be drawn in free-hand, using a ballpoint pen for outlining and a marker in the same colour for filling in (see fig. 1). Powder the drawing with talcum powder when the marker ink is dry to give it a matt appearance (see fig. 2).

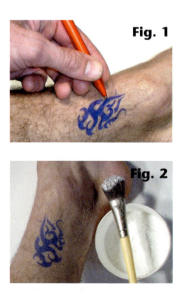

Fig. 1

Fig. 2

Freehand with cream or water-based make-up

Materials:
Rough sketch of tattoo, cream or water-based make-up (black, and selected colours), brushes, water-repellent face powder, fixer spray for use on skin.

Draw the tattoo in freehand using cream or water-based make-up. It's best to use a thin, stiff brush to get nice even lines. Water-based make-up is the easiest to work with but by its very nature is not water-repellent; cream make-up is water-resistant and goes further but is more greasy to work with (see figs 3 and 4).

When you have finished drawing the tattoo, apply a thin layer of face powder to the whole drawing. Then carefully brush the powder away with a powder brush, leaving the drawing a matt colour (see fig. 5). Touch up the drawing and apply another layer of powder, repeating this procedure until you are satisfied with the results. You can also spray the tattoo with fixer spray; this will make the tattoo shiny and more durable, but don't apply too much as it can form a film which will crack. If you want the tattoo to look old and matt, finish off by powdering and brushing again (see fig. 6).

For this method, you can also use self-adhesive wax templates, which are available in various patterns and pictures from tattoo shops. Press the template onto the skin until it sticks. Carefully dab paint onto the template and powder as described above.

Tattoo stamp

Materials:

A potato, plasticine or wax plate for casting teeth, a knife or surgical knife, water-based or cream make-up (the colour of your choice – tattoos are usually black or dark blue).

If you are going to use a tattoo several times – for instance, in a film or TV recording – it may be a good idea to make a tattoo stamp so that the tattoo looks the same each time.

Cut out the motif on a half potato, a lump of plasticine or a wax plate. Cover the stamp with a layer of cream or water-based make-up, and press it against the skin. Then powder the tattoo lightly until you get a matt surface.

Fig. 3

Fig. 4

Fig. 5

Fig. 6

Make plenty of rough sketches so you are well prepared when you start drawing the actual tattoos.

Various skin ailments can be made-up quite easily, and are mainly used for film characters and photos advertising skin products.

Materials:
Latex, brushes, spatula, Vaseline, mayonnaise, theatrical blood, derma wax, gelatine powder, Tuplast, cream make-up (yellow, red, brown), porridge oats or desiccated coconut, hairdryer.

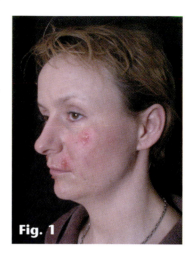

Fig. 1

When a person has spots or acne, it's because the skin produces too much fatty tallow. The tallow reacts with air to form black blockages of the skin pores (blackheads). Accumulated tallow, dead skin cells and bacteria cause inflammation which develops into pimples, in severe cases also termed acne. Skin ailments can be rashes, spots or areas of infected skin. Eczema appears as reddish skin with small blisters that cause the skin to ooze and scabs to form when they burst. Psoriasis is a red or pink, dry rash with a silvery, scaly surface. It is most commonly found on the elbows, knees, shins, scalp and the lower part of the back.

Spots with derma wax
Take a small piece of derma wax about the size of a pimple. Massage it until soft and put it onto the desired place using the pointed end of the spatula. Smooth the edges so you get a small mound. Tint around the pimples with red cream make-up (see fig. 1).

Eczema and rashes
Light eczema can be made-up with a little reddish cream make-up, toned onto the skin. To simulate flaky skin, apply a single layer of

latex and dry with a hairdryer. Scratch the surface of the latex with your nail or the pointed end of a spatula to make it look like peeling skin. Tone around the affected area, and where the skin has peeled off, with a little red cream make-up.

Pimples with latex
Apply small specks of latex or lukewarm gelatine mixture to the face, using the pointed end of the spatula. Don't overdo it, and place them randomly; pimples do not form symmetrically or in patterns. Dry with a hairdryer (using cold air if you use gelatine), and then apply more latex or gelatine on top of the pimples to make them bigger. Repeat this procedure until the pimples are of an appropriate size (see fig. 2). Tone lightly with red cream make-up around the spots (see fig. 3), but be careful – it mustn't look 'painted'. You can make pimples appear to have burst by applying a little dash of mayonnaise or butter on top of them. For a

more severe case, tone the skin surrounding the pimples redder (see fig. 4). If you want actual scabs, colour brownish or dark red around the pimples (see fig. 5).

Cold sores

Dab a little latex near the mouth. Allow it to dry partially and then put a little porridge oats, desiccated coconut or something

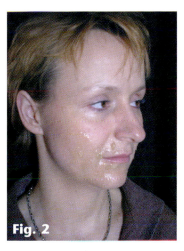

Fig. 2

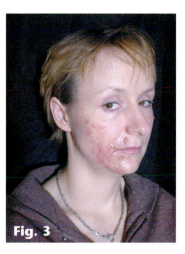

Fig. 3

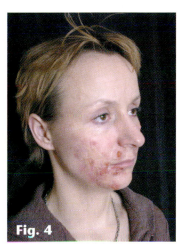

Fig. 4

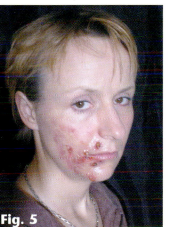

Fig. 5

similar onto the latex and apply another layer of latex on top. Leave to dry. Colour with brownish, yellowish and reddish cream make-up and a little theatrical blood. For suppurating cold sores, apply a little Vaseline. This effect can also be achieved using derma wax, gelatine or Tuplast.

For colour photos of various skin ailments, I recommend professional literature and medical magazines. Glaxo, for example, produces an information series about skin diseases.

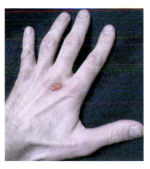
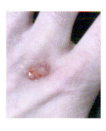

The skin disease basal cell cancer. This effect can be created with Tuplast coloured with a little theatrical blood.

Blood, cerebral tissue, vomit, slime – and that which is worse still. These unpleasant things are common ingredients in violent, horror and sci-fi films, and they can all be made with things from your own kitchen.

Artificial blood

Ketchup is no good for this: it's too thick and has the wrong colour. A better alternative is thickened cherry sauce.

There are many ways of making homemade blood. If you only need small amounts, the best thing is to simply use ready-made theatrical blood. An alternative blood dye is blood-powder, which you can get from theatre make-up shops. If you want a slightly thicker blood-substance, mix the powder with gelatine and boiling water. If the mixture becomes too light a colour, mix in some soy sauce, gravy colouring or dark syrup.

Red fruit colouring has a good colour for blood but is difficult to wash off skin, clothes and wooden floors. It is very cheap, though, and can be mixed with a little glycerine or cornflour to get a thicker consistency. Alternatively, you can mix the fruit colouring with golden syrup. Find the best proportions by experimenting a bit.

Brains

Mix the following ingredients in a bowl: mashed banana, liver pâté, porridge, rich cleansing lotion and a little gelatine. Experiment with the proportions and leave the resulting substance to thicken a bit after you've finished. Apply the cerebral substance where needed and sprinkle a little theatrical blood over it.

Vomit

Put a small portion of porridge in a bowl and add a few peas, maize and pieces of diced carrot. Then mix in a little syrup or soy sauce, to make it darker. You can also add a little sugar to make it taste a bit better! The actor puts the mixture in his or her mouth with a tablespoon and spits it out again to simulate vomiting.

Pus and slime

The best way to make slime is to heat powdered gelatine and water, and mix it into a thin, slimy porridge. Then stir in a little colouring to get the desired effect; this could be theatrical blood, watercolour or liquid, water-based make-up. Note, however, that the gelatine stiffens when it goes cold.

Another method is to make slime out of glycerine, Vaseline and a little colouring, all mixed together. Clear liquid soap can also be used, running from the jaws of a monster, for instance.

Mayonnaise quite closely resembles pus, suppurating pimples and other impurities of the skin. Apply it to the desired location with the tip of a spatula.

Tears

Dab a little glycerine beneath the eye under the tear duct so that it runs down the cheeks. (Be careful not to get it into the eyes.) However, nothing beats real tears: very sparingly apply a little onion juice from a cut

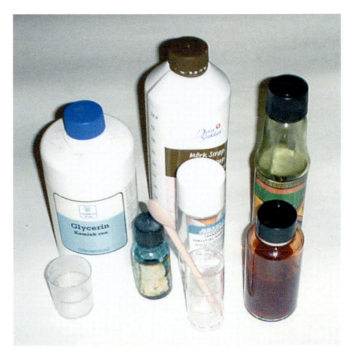

With a mixture of food from your fridge and products from under your kitchen sink, you can concoct the most distasteful substances.

onion, or a very small amount of tiger balm, below the eye. This will most certainly make the eyes water. But be careful not to get it in your eyes, especially tiger balm, as this can be very painful.

You can also buy a tear stick in a cylinder. This contains a eucalyptus cream and is applied directly below the eyes.

Semen
Mix raw egg whites with a little white watercolour paint – or another kind of liquid, water-based paint.

Sweat
Apply glycerine with a cotton bud or an eyedropper so that it forms little pearls of 'sweat' – for instance, along the hairline, and on the forehead and temples. To achieve a very sweaty look, apply plain water to the hair, armpits and on the back between the shoulder blades. You can also buy artificial sweat such as *Transparent Jelly*, manufactured by Kryolan.

Faeces
Make a very thick porridge and mix in soy sauce, gravy colouring, coffee, cocoa powder and other brown things. Mix it all well until you achieve the desired texture and colour.

Crepe hair, also called crepe wool hair, is used for artificial beards and hair. It is usually sold in small plaits tied with string and comes in many different colours. The hair fibres are 2–3 cm long and stick to each other because they have microscopic barbs: real hairs are not barbed in this way, but display a palm-like structure when viewed through a microscope.

Crepe wool hair is naturally fuzzy but can be straightened by ironing the hair through a damp cloth or by scalding it in hot water. Loosen the string, and a lock of hair will unfold like a fan (see fig. 1). Carefully pull out the desired length of hair until the lock loosens itself. To prepare the hair, separate the hairs in the lock lengthwise and bring them together again several times. Gradually, the hair will even out and become straighter. Natural hair seldom has just one colour, so during this process you can mix several hair colours together.

Fig. 1

Artificial beard

Materials:
Mastix, latex or Stoppelpaste, prepared crepe hair, scissors.

If the model has more than one day's worth of bristles, shave them. Cut the crepe hair into pieces of the desired length and apply Stoppelpaste, latex or mastix to the area where you want to affix the beard. Avoid getting mastix or latex too close to the model's real hair, as it can be difficult to get out again. When the mastix or latex is semi-dry, mount the locks of crepe hair one by one in rows, starting from the bottom and moving upwards so that each row of crepe hair covers the glue of the row beneath it. When you get to the top and final row, puff the hair slightly to conceal the glue seam. Now you can carefully trim the beard with a pair of scissors.

Artificial bristles 1

Materials:
Mastix or Stoppelpaste, leftover bits of crepe hair, scissors, towel, brush, talcum powder.

Cut some locks of crepe hair into tiny bits the length of bristles, and collect them in a small container. Place a towel over the shoulders of the model. Apply Stoppelpaste or mastix to the model's chin, and sprinkle the little bristles onto it. If you use mastix, powder the chin very lightly with talcum powder, when the mastix is dry.

Artificial bristles 2

Materials:
Bristle-sponge, black and brownish cream make-up.

Carefully apply a little black or brown-black cream make-up to a bristle-sponge. Then dab the model's chin lightly with the sponge where you want the bristles to appear. Be careful not to overdo it.

Artificial eyebrows

Materials:
Stoppelpaste, flexible sealer, cream make-up in skin-colours, brushes, mastix, prepared crepe hair, scissors.

Run a Stoppelpaste stick along the eyebrows so that the eyebrow hairs are flattened. Then apply a layer of flexible sealer, which works just like matt lacquer – protecting the hairs and giving a smooth surface. The lacquer takes a little while to dry.

When the sealer is dry, paint the eyebrow area with cream make-up, mixed to a colour that matches the colour of the skin. When the eyebrows are no longer visible, apply a line of mastix to the area where the new brow is going to be (avoid getting mastix in the eyes). When the mastix is semi-dry, mount the wool crepe, either in small pieces placed in a row or as one longer piece, curled up. When the mastix is completely dry, trim the false eyebrow into shape with a pair of scissors.

Artificial beard on tulle

Materials:
Eye pencil, baking paper, skin-coloured tulle, ballpoint pen, scissors, mastix or latex, prepared crepe hair, a spatula, a disposable brush or other utensil (optional).

Draw the outline of a beard on the model with an eye pencil. Make a template out of baking paper by placing it over the beard and drawing the outline on the paper. You can also draw directly on the tulle. Now cut out a piece of tulle in the shape of the beard. Test the beard piece on the model and cut it to size. If you want a chin-beard, you can fold the tulle so you get a hollow for the chin. The folded part can be glued together with mastix or latex, or you can stitch it together (see fig. 2).

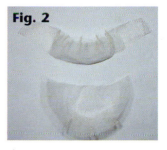

Fig. 2

Prepare some crepe hair and cut it to the right length. It's a good idea to mix several colours of crepe hair, to get a more realistic colour for the beard. Now place the piece of tulle on an oilcloth, a wooden board or any other surface you don't mind getting bits of glue on. Paint a line with mastix or latex: for latex, use a spatula, disposable brush or simply your finger. Affix small pieces of prepared crepe hair in rows – working upwards from the bottom – with each row slightly overlapping the one below. At the top and final row, puff up the hair a bit to cover the glue seam. Leave the mastix or latex to dry, and then loosen it carefully from the working surface. It may stick a bit; if so, ease it off with the spatula.

Carefully trim the beard with a pair of scissors while it's still on the model or glass bust (see fig. 3). Now your artificial beard is ready for use and you can glue it to your model with mastix or latex.

Fig. 3

To remove the beard, simply ease it off carefully. If you glued it with mastix, you can take it off using mastix-remover: dip a cotton bud in the solution and hold the bud on the mastix for a few seconds until the glue has dissolved. Do this carefully and slowly, as mastix-remover is a strong solvent and may irritate the skin. Latex or mastix cannot be

removed from crepe hair; you have to cut off the leftover bits, and then the remaining hair can be re-used.

Mounting crepe hair and whiskers on masks and bald caps

Materials:
Prepared crepe hair, scissors, latex in a little bowl, a mask or bald cap.

If you want a mask resembling the face of an animal, or maybe a troll, you can affix crepe hair to look like a beard, facial hair, eyebrows and whiskers. Pull a lock of crepe hair straight repeatedly, to straighten out the hair. Mix different colours to get a natural-looking shade. Cut the prepared hair into small pieces about 1 cm in length, so that every piece has a blunt end. Dip the blunt ends carefully in the latex and mount them one by one on the mask or bald cap, moving upwards from the bottom and pushing them together so that the hairs are placed closely together. If you want a pattern or variation in hair colour, you must sort the pieces into different lengths and colours before starting. When all the hair is mounted, dry the latex and trim the hair with scissors if necessary.

Whiskers can be bought ready-made, or you can use some hairs from a brush. The brush hairs are slightly thicker than real whiskers, but they'll still do. Dip one end of the whisker in latex and stick it to the mask.

Making artificial beards and wigs by plugging

Materials:
Eye pencil, baking paper, skin-coloured tulle, plugging needle, locks of real hair, sewing thread of same colour as the tulle (optional).

This method requires a great deal of time and patience. In return, you get professional looking wigs and beard-pieces. Draw the desired beard on the model or onto a glass bust, using a pencil. Make a template on a piece of translucent paper, e.g. baking paper, and cut a piece of tulle to the shape of the template. Try out the piece of tulle on the model or glass bust. If the beard is a chin-beard, fold the tulle, thereby creating a hollow for the chin. Stitch the folded part together with a piece of thread of the same colour as the tulle. Cut pieces of real hair in the chosen colour to the right length. Fold 3–4 strands of hair around the head of the plugging needle and stick them through the netting of the tulle. Tie the hairs to the tulle with a knot. Continue this process until the whole beard or wig is finished.

In films and plays, actors sometimes have to appear to be bald – or to have less than their natural head of hair, for instance, if they're playing the part of a monk or a samurai. In such cases you use a bald cap, which is like a skin-coloured bathing cap. (If you want the opposite effect – i.e. the actor having more hair – you simply use a wig.)

Making a bald cap

> **Materials:**
> Glass or plastic bust, latex or glatzan, disposable brush, washing-up liquid, glass bowls, hairdryer, face powder or talcum powder.

To make a bald cap you use latex or glatzan. Latex gives a softer and more supple bald cap; glatzan gives a more durable bald cap, which is also thinner and therefore gives a less visible borderline. However, glatzan is the more expensive of the two and requires good ventilation while working with it, as it has a very strong odour.

A bald cap is made over a glass or plastic bust. If you use a plastic bust, you must first rub the scalp lightly with sandpaper to remove any grooves and other irregularities. If working with glatzan, apply a thin layer of Vaseline to the scalp before you start. The pictures show the making of a latex bald cap.

Pour latex or glatzan into a little bowl and apply it to the bust using a brush. Start with the edges of the bald cap, i.e. around the forehead, above the ears and all the way round the back of the neck. Then cover the whole of the scalp and dry with a hairdryer (see fig. 1). It is important that the edge of

the bald cap is very thin, as this makes it easier to conceal the borderline when the cap is worn. For this reason, each layer of latex or glatzen should start 1 cm from the edge of the first layer. Using this method, apply 5–6 layers of latex or glatzen to get a durable bald cap, which will stand up to being used again and again (see fig. 2). After repeated use, however, the edges will become jagged and need to be repaired. It is also important that you make the bald cap extra long down the back of the neck, as there is a lot of strain on this area.

If you want your bald cap to have a colour, you can mix liquid water-based paint or special latex paint into the latex prior to use. Then, simply make the bald cap using the coloured latex. However, you can also colour the latex bald cap afterwards using cream or water-based make-up.

When the final layer is dry, powder the entire bald cap with face powder or talcum powder. Carefully, loosen the cap from the forehead using your nails or a spatula. Then carefully push some face powder or talcum powder underneath the cap, and ease it off while powdering continuously (see fig. 3). If you don't powder it, the bald cap will stick to itself and be extremely difficult to separate again. Once a finished bald cap has been thoroughly powdered, it will not be harmed by soap and water and is ready for use (see fig. 4). If there are loose shreds around the edges, simply cut them off.

Advice on the use of brushes

Never use expensive, quality brushes for latex or glatzan, as both products are very difficult to remove from brush hairs. Instead, use disposable brushes. However, in order to be able to use the same brush throughout the job, there are certain precautions you can take – such as dipping the brush in soapy water before use (the soap prevents the wet latex from drying). Every time you're not using the brush, place it in the soapy water. The small amounts of soap that are left on the brush, and therefore get onto the bust, will not prevent the latter from drying. If working with glatzan, clean the brush first in acetone, then in soapy water, before using it.

When working with latex, you can also use a spatula or a sponge. The sponge will dry hard after use and you will not be able to clean it. However, it is also possible to use a foam dishcloth: dip it in latex and apply the latex to the bust. The latter method results in a more airy latex, which also dries faster.

Fig. 2

Fig. 3

Fig. 4

Fig. 1

Putting on the bald cap

> **Materials:**
> Scissors, ballpoint pen, mastix, prostick or latex.
>
> The following items are optional: hairnet or nylon stocking, mastix-remover and cotton buds, water atomizer.

Note: When putting the bald cap on your model, you want the model's hair to take up as little space as possible. You can use a water atomizer to flatten it; if the model has long hair, dampen it and comb it round the head like a turban. Alternatively, you can use a hairnet or nylon stocking to hold the hair down.

If the model has long hair, dampen it, comb it round the head like a turban and squash it flat.

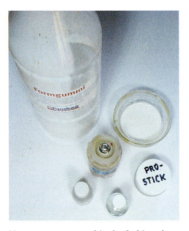

You can use any kind of skin glue as long as it has elastic properties. Latex is a good choice, for this reason.

Adjustments

Pull the bald cap carefully over the model's head and cut it to size using a pair of scissors. It should go down to the middle of the forehead and well down the back of the neck. Leave at least 2 cm of bald cap below the hairline at the back of the neck for a glue seam. Cut the edges carefully while the model is wearing the bald cap, or draw the contour with a pen and cut with the cap off the model. Cut semicircular holes for the ears, to allow for adjustment of the cap. The bald cap should go approximately 1–1.5 cm below the hairline to leave room for a seam of glue all the way round.

Glue

To glue the bald cap on, you can use mastix, latex, prostick or any other skin glue. Latex is perhaps the best choice, especially round the back of the neck, as latex is elastic when dry. The area at the back of the neck on the bald cap is always placed under great strain when the model moves their head.

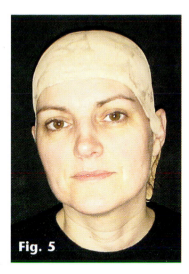
Fig. 5

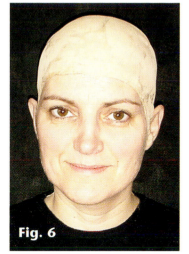
Fig. 6

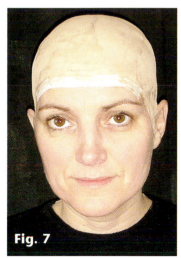
Fig. 7

Fitting the bald cap

Pull the bald cap over the scalp and adjust it, tucking away any hair that may be sticking out (see fig. 5). Start gluing at the forehead. Apply skin glue to the inside edge of the cap's forehead, about a 0.5 cm in. Leave the glue to dry for about 20 seconds and then press the cap firmly against the forehead. You can also ask the model to hold it in place until the glue is completely dry. Now continue gluing around one side of the cap and then the other, in the same manner. When both sides are glued, pull the cap firmly down the back of the neck and glue there too – making sure that it is securely fixed, or it may flop loose when the model moves her head.

When the bald cap is on and all the glue is dry (see fig. 6), check all the edges. If parts of the edge show too much – which is often the case with a bald cap that has been used several times – you can conceal these with a little latex and toilet paper. Cut toilet paper into thin strips and mount them with a little latex to smooth the transition between cap and skin (see fig. 7). When the latex is dry, the edges should be less visible.

The bald cap is now ready for colouring. This can be done with an airbrush, a brush or a sponge. You can use foundation, camouflage make-up or water-based, cream or rubber make-up.

Taking the cap off

To remove the bald cap, carefully loosen the edge around the forehead or temples. Ease the cap free, little by little. If you've used mastix, carefully dissolve the glue with mastix-remover on a cotton bud. Slowly peel off the latex, which won't be dissolved by the mastix-remover. Be careful round the hairline and where there are fine hairs on the skin, as it may hurt to have glue and latex pulled off such areas. You should leave the back of the neck until last; there's a good chance that the bald cap will stick to the fine hairs there.

When you have taken off the bald cap, remove bits of glue and latex from the edges. If you have used gelatine or other perishable materials, rinse these off, and the bald cap is ready to be used again. It may be a good idea to turn the bald cap inside out and put it to dry in the airing cupboard after use, as there will be sweat and condensation on the inside.

Repairing a bald cap

If a bald cap has holes or the edges have become frayed, carefully mount it on a glass or plastic bust: it must be taut around the areas to be repaired. Carefully apply 2–3 layers of latex to the repair area. Let the latex dry thoroughly, and powder well before use.

Building onto a bald cap

Mount the finished bald cap on a glass or plastic bust, and you can model it into a new project: alien being, Frankenstein's monster, cone-head, fractured skull effect or something completely different. A good method is to model with pieces of cotton wool dipped in latex, or you can use other latex parts to model a completely new cap. Try to avoid making the cap too big and heavy, though, as this may make it difficult to put the cap on.

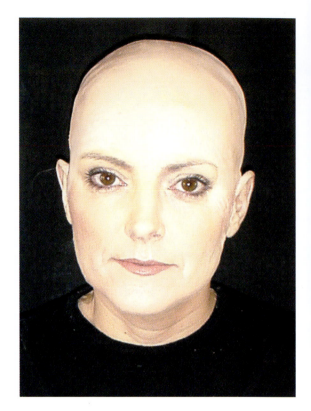

When making up a younger person to look older, it's a good idea to study what it is that makes people look old.

People age differently depending on factors such as genes, race, personality, lifestyle, diet, and the environment in which they live. The lines of the face reflect a person's character and temperament. Lines created by joy and laughter look different from lines created by anger, frustration, illness and suffering. By exploiting this fact, you can make up a fictive personality. For instance, a person who has led a very unhealthy life, smoked heavily, sunbathed too much or been out in the wind and rain a lot, will have a more haggard skin than a person who has led a healthy lifestyle and taken good care of themselves.

Ageing someone realistically with make-up requires some knowledge of the sinews and muscles of the face, as these determine how the skin sags and falls in. Emphasise lines and hollows with dark or brownish shadows, and highlight raised areas with light make-up. A thin face can be made to look older by emphasising wrinkles and hollows; a full and broad face can be aged by emphasising loose skin and double chins.

There are several ways to age someone using make-up. The method described below is best suited for theatre and other situations where a person will be viewed from a distance. Ageing using latex, on the other hand, will also work close-up. The most effective ageing method is to make a mask out of latex foam, but this is outside the scope of this book.

Ageing a face using make-up

Materials:
Sponges and brushes, foundation, white cake make-up, eye shadow (brownish tints, white, grey-black, blue-grey), red eye pencil, cream make-up (red, white, yellow, brown).

If it is necessary to alter the model's skin colour, to make it either paler or darker, colour the face with foundation or with a very thin layer of white transparent cake make-up (see fig. 1). Study the model's face and decide which wrinkles would look natural. When drawing lines and wrinkles use brownish and grey-black eye-shadow colours, which emphasise hollows (see fig. 2). Whitish shading, or highlight, emphasises raised areas. For normal light conditions, lay the darker shadow below the line.

Make up the following details and shadows: bags under the eyes; heavy eyelids; wrinkles on the bridge of the nose; wrinkles from the corners of the eyes; forehead wrinkles; sunken temple shadow; wrinkles on cheeks going from the wings of the nose down past the mouth; hollow cheek shadow; shadow below the lower lip; small wrinkles on the lips; double chin.

If the facial wrinkles are too 'hard' and conspicuous, apply a very fine layer of foundation or colourless cake make-up with a sponge. Colour directly below the lower eyelashes with a red eyeliner pencil, or tone with red cream make-up (see fig. 3). Tone the eyebrows and hairline grey or whitish with white cake make-up, cream or water-based make-up. Dab lightly with a little red cream make-up on a bristle-sponge to simulate tiny, broken veins under the skin. Paint liver spots around the temples using a mix of yellow and brown make-up. Fine veins can be drawn using blue-green eye shadow. Use a liquid eyeliner brush.

If you want your model to look like someone who has been angry all their life, emphasise the horizontal lines between the eyebrows. Tone the eye hollows dark with shadow, and tone horizontal wrinkles and bags under the eyes. Emphasise lines around the corners of the mouth. If you want to model a happy person who has smiled all their life, emphasise the wrinkles in the outer corner of the eyes and smiling lines around the mouth.

Fig. 1

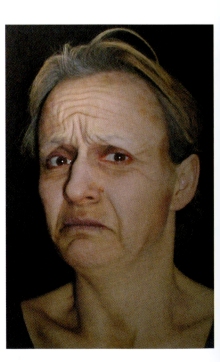

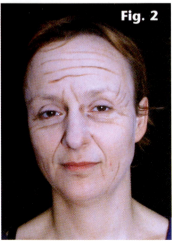

Fig. 2

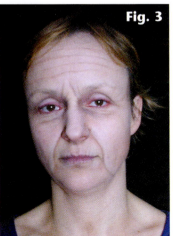

Fig. 3

To make the make-up more convincing, you must also include the neck. Tone with a dark shadow in the hollow between the collarbones, and emphasise the muscle, which runs obliquely from behind the ears down to the collarbones. A pair of old-fashioned glasses, a stick and clothes typically worn by elderly people will round off the ageing effect nicely.

Ageing using latex

Using make-up, simulate the major wrinkles in the same way as described above: bags under the eyes, lines on the cheeks and around the corners of the mouth.

Now, think of how the muscles and sinews run on the face, and where the skin will wrinkle, sag or be tight. Stretch the skin across the direction of muscles and sinews using two fingers. Then lay a line of latex on the skin along the direction of the muscles and sinews using a spatula or disposable brush. Avoid getting latex in the eyes or too close to hair, eyebrows and nostrils. Dry with a hairdryer while keeping the skin pulled out (be careful not to hold the hairdryer too

close so that you burn the person's skin.) When the latex is dry and translucent, let go of the skin. Pinch the skin lightly together against the direction of stretch, and it will wrinkle slightly. Repeat this procedure 2–3 times on top of the same line of latex until you get the desired level of wrinkling (see fig. 4).

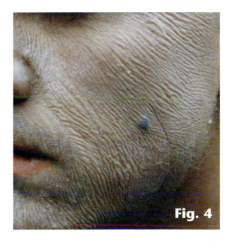

Fig. 4

Treat the whole face and neck, and if necessary the hands, in the same way. The effect works best when used on skin that is already loose, as the latex will then contract and wrinkle more when released. When the work is finished, powder the made-up area with face powder or talc.

There will be a conspicuous transition from latex to skin, which can be concealed with skin-coloured crème stick or cream make-up, carefully blended in with a brush. Finally, powder lightly. Carefully colour the ridge beneath the lower eyelashes using a red eye pencil and tone using a brush. This will give the impression of a pair of tired, old eyes.

Tone eyebrows and the hairline grey or whitish using white cake, cream or water-based make-up. Liver spots can be painted using a mix of yellow and brown cream make-up. Dry the model's teeth with a piece of kitchen roll, then paint them nicotine-yellow using yellow tooth lacquer. Leave the tooth lacquer to dry for a minute or so before the model closes their mouth.

A grey or white wig, a walking stick, a pair of glasses and a set of clothes typically worn by elderly people will round off the effect. Furthermore, special-effects contact lenses (for instance, white blind eyes or matt grey cataract lenses) may be used for additional effect.

Ageing hands

Materials:

Softputty or derma wax, a piece of thin plastic from a carrier bag, a spatula or wooden cosmetics spatula, latex, tissue paper or plain kitchen roll, hairdryer, cream make-up (reddish-brown, yellow, skin-coloured, brown, red).

Roll 28 little pieces of softputty or derma wax into balls. Place the balls on the joints of the fingers and knuckles and press them flat. Lay a thin piece of plastic over the top and scrape lines in the wax with a spatula or a little wooden stick. Look at the other hand to get an idea of how the lines around the joints and knuckles run. Remove the plastic (see fig. 5).

Apply latex to a small area around the joints and knuckles, and lay tissue paper or a piece of kitchen roll over the latex (see fig. 6). Press the latex and paper down lightly and dry with a hairdryer. Crumple the paper a little and apply more latex on top. Dry with a hairdryer again and crumple the paper till the wrinkles are right. This method will give very wrinkled hands (see fig. 7). If you're going for a more moderate effect, leave out the paper.

Colour the lines in the wax using reddish-brown cream make-up. Colour the rest of the hand with yellow, skin-coloured and brown cream make-up, and tone slightly red around the nails (see fig. 8). You could also affix crepe hair to the hand to simulate natural hair growth.

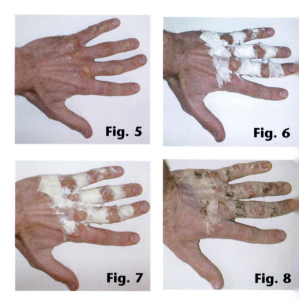

Fig. 5

Fig. 6

Fig. 7

Fig. 8

Shock make-up can be used in most cases where injuries are involved, and for horror films. If someone has been shot, had their foot smashed, witnessed a traffic accident or something else, it is important to make the person look shocked. Whether on stage or in a film, if the person is smiling and looking relaxed, it's going to ruin the effect.

Materials:

Make-up sponge, brushes, white cake make-up, red eye pencil, eye shadow (brown-grey), glycerine.

Make the skin a pallid colour with whitish cake make-up. Draw a red line on the ridge below the eyes. Shadow lightly below the eyes, round the area where you tend to get bags and wrinkles. Dab glycerine onto the upper lip, cheekbones and forehead along the hairline. Tell the model to assume a staring gaze.

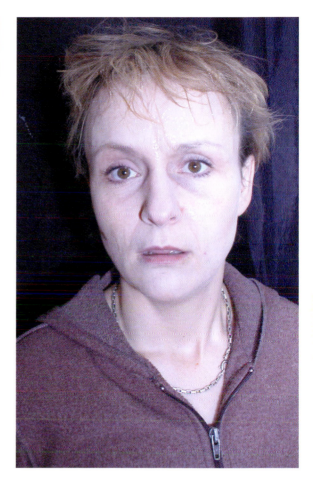

If you want an actor to look dead, it's important that the skin has an appropriate colour. The skin of a corpse turns pale because the blood coagulates in the veins – or, in the case of violent death, it has left the body. When the causes of death are natural, the person may get jaundice while dying which makes the skin turn a yellowish hue.

Materials:
Make-up sponge, brushes, white cake make-up, red eye pencil, eye shadow (brown-grey), glycerine.

Corpse with a yellowish hue.

Make up the actor's skin using translucent white on a sponge. You're not making up Pierrot, so don't make the skin too white – just tone it pale: a translucent cake make-up mixed with a little water is fine. If you want the skin a cadaverous yellow, use a light-yellow cream make-up. Remember to make up the neck, hands and arms too, if these are going to be visible.

Lay reddish and brownish shadows around the eyes, to give the illusion of sunken-in eyes. You can also lay a little brown-grey shadow on the cheeks, to make them look hollow. Tone the lips slightly blue with cream make-up mixed with a little lipgloss or Vaseline.

Corpse with a generally pale hue.

If you want the corpse to have liver spots, make these up as brownish or bluish blots, in the same way as you would bruises (see the section on bruises, page 52).

It is said that the eyes are the windows of the soul: so, if they look different from how you expect, the effect can be both scary and weird.

I have suggested lenses of some sort for quite a few of the effects described in this book. You can buy special effects lenses such as cat's eyes, blind eyes, grey cataract eyes, spiral eyes, evil eyes with no iris, crazy eyes with symbols in them like a dollar sign, a skull, a smiley, or a heart. You can even get lenses identical to those used in particular films like *Interview with a Vampire, The Lost Boys, Dracula* and others. Special effects contact lenses can be bought from opticians or ordered over the Internet.

If you want lenses made according to your own personal design, from a sketch or a drawing, this can be done: contact a lens laboratory through an optician. However, these personalised lenses will cost you quite a bit more than the mass-produced ones. You can get both hard and soft lenses, though the hard ones are rarely used these days and most special effects lenses and ordinary contact lenses are soft.

When you buy any kind of contact lenses, you have to have an eye test. Among other things, the eye is measured so that you get a lens suited to your individual requirements. For hygienic reasons, lenses are strictly personal and I strongly advise against trying on someone else's. Furthermore, special effects lenses should not be used more than about 30 times. Store the lenses according to the optician's guidelines.

Some special effects lenses – for instance cat's eyes or dollar-signs and skulls – have to

be the right way up to look convincing. The vertical cat's pupil can simply 'topple over' if the lens isn't positioned properly, which will confuse rather than give the desired dramatic effect. However, most types of lenses are constructed in such a way that they adjust after you have blinked a couple of times, and experienced lens-users can adjust the lens by simply rotating it with a finger.

If you don't normally use contact lenses, it may take a few days for your eyes to get used to wearing them. Therefore, it is a good idea to let an actor wear and become accustomed to the lenses, prior to the recording of a film or opening night of a play. Always carry a lens case and some sterile salt-water in case you need to remove the lenses.

If you order lenses over the Internet, make sure you do it through an optician who can vouch for their safety. It is illegal for a lens manufacturer to sell directly to customers without an authorised optician or eye doctor approving the product. You can find a wide range of fantastic and imaginative special effects lenses by entering the keywords 'special effects lenses'. Among the more unusual lenses are: mirror lenses, UV-fluorescent lenses and lenses which cover the entire eye (the latter are said to be unpleasant to wear).

Advice on the use of contact lenses
If your lens feels uncomfortable, carefully push it to one side with your finger and then

push it back again. This will usually do the
trick. If it still irritates the eye, take it out and
rinse it in saline which you can buy at an
opticians. Never put a ruined or damaged
lens in your eye; it can harm the eye's retina –
and never use old lenses, as this will increase
the risk of complications. Only sleep with
lenses in if your optician recommends that
your lenses are suitable for this.

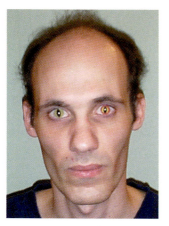
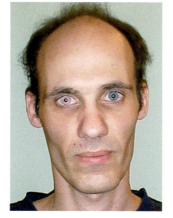

Here are four different types of special effects lenses.

These lenses are by the makers of
Crazy Lenses.

Today, advanced body-painting is frequently seen in adverts, art exhibitions and music videos. Modern body-paint is allergy tested and allows skin to breathe so that even complex designs can be created safely.

Classic body-paint

The naked body presents an excellent canvas for the artist to paint on. Body-painting clothes is all about deceiving the eye. Painted clothes inevitably have to depict tight-fitting garments, but a little shadow and painted effects can give the impression of folds and creases. Actually, it's best to exaggerate a little, as the eye is willingly deceived by the illusion of painted clothes.

It's a good idea to make sketches to work from, before you start painting – both to get an overview of the entire work, and also to have been through the body-painting once and know where the difficulties lie. Start by drawing the outlines and marking where the sleeves and collar end. Use a light liquid eyeliner brush or a narrow brush with a little light colour on. Then fill out the major, larger areas using a wide brush or a sponge. Finally, paint in effects such as shading, stitches and seams, pockets, folds and creases.

Look at a shirt on a model or in a photo to see how clothes actually fold. Note that where clothes bulge out, the colour will be lighter than on areas where the material hollows, creating a darker area. These differences in colour can be simulated by mixing black and white colour into the painted base-colour. Seams can be painted with a thin brush. Where the sleeves and the collar meet the skin, you get a little shadow: paint a thin black line – and on the skin side, a light brown shadow line. Tone this brown line with a damp clean brush, blurring the transition to the skin. A fun effect can be to affix buttons to a shirt or jacket, or glue a handkerchief onto a painted pocket.

Body-paint for commercial purposes

Body-paint can be used to advertise a company's logo, slogan or product. Commercial body-paint is used at exhibitions, in shops and shopping centres, and in ordinary commercial photography for magazines and posters. Usually, the client wants a company uniform, a t-shirt or a jacket with the company logo painted on a model. Make several drafts when selling a concept to a company. Ask for some material with the company logo so you have something to work from. Cut the logo out in cardboard and make a template to paint through. Practise drawing the logo freehand if you're not using a template; it's imperative that the client's logo or text is painted clearly.

It's a good idea to bring some sweets or chocolate for the model, as it can be very tiring to stand still for 2–3 hours. Ask the model to bring a dressing gown or something similar so they don't have to walk partially or totally naked onto the stage. Also ask them to bring underwear in the right colour (or buy a pair for the model yourself), as fabric absorbs paint making it difficult to paint on. Don't forget to bring your own camera so you can take photos of your work; at exhibitions, the clients don't always take their own photos. In the case of public body-painting there should be a barrier at least 1 metre around the model, marking how close the audience is allowed to go.

Fantasy body-paint

A fairy tale with paint and brushes. Who says body-paint has to be restricted to suits, t-shirts and shirts? Body-painting can also depict: the deep sea with fish, a jungle with trees, leaves and wild animals, a space monster, a bowl of fruit, musical instruments, abstract art, etc. Use the contours of the body as inspiration. The imagination should work unhindered. For instance, you could paint a model so that he/she blends into the background in the same way as a chameleon.

Ethics

Body-painting is an intimate art form – in fact, this is the whole magic of it. Therefore, it is important that you respect the model, who is placing their body in your hands. If the model is a woman, paint the breasts first so that she feels her nudity less. It is also about respecting your audience, for instance, elderly people who may be passing by. Try to avoid people taking photos without your and the model's permission.

Airbrush

An airbrush consists of an air-compressor, a spray gun and a container for liquid water-based paint. The compressors come in various sizes and prices, from £50 ($80) to £1800 ($2800). You often buy the gun separately, and there are several different types.

The 'spreader' has two functions. You regulate the air pressure by pressing it down, and by pulling it back you regulate the amount of paint coming out of the nozzle. Press the spreader lightly, and get a feeling of how much paint it takes to make a nice shadow. The closer you hold the nozzle to the surface, the finer a line you get, and the less air-pressure you want. The further you hold the nozzle from the surface, the larger an area you will cover. You should have the air-pressure on maximum when painting from a distance. With an airbrush, you can achieve fine highlights, and shadowing and toning effects. Using templates cut from cardboard, paper or plastic, you can achieve impressive results. The same applies to lace and netting used as templates.

The outer parts of the gun can be screwed off to adjust the field of spray – this will expose the needle. Be careful not to knock the tip of the spray gun against something hard; the small needle at the end of the nozzle bends easily, and if this happens it can't be used any more and must be replaced.

The paint goes in the gun's container. Never use anything but liquid water-based paint, or you'll block the nozzle. Glitter-paint and similar products are not suited for an airbrush, as these will also block the nozzle.

Use cut-out cardboard, paper or plastic templates to spray through, or use tulle, lace, frills and various net structures to create pretty patterns.

Always clean the nozzle after use, as dried-out paint will accumulate in the barrel and nozzle. Rinse it through by using water instead of paint. You can also use a special airbrush cleaner, but don't use shampoo, as it will just start foaming.

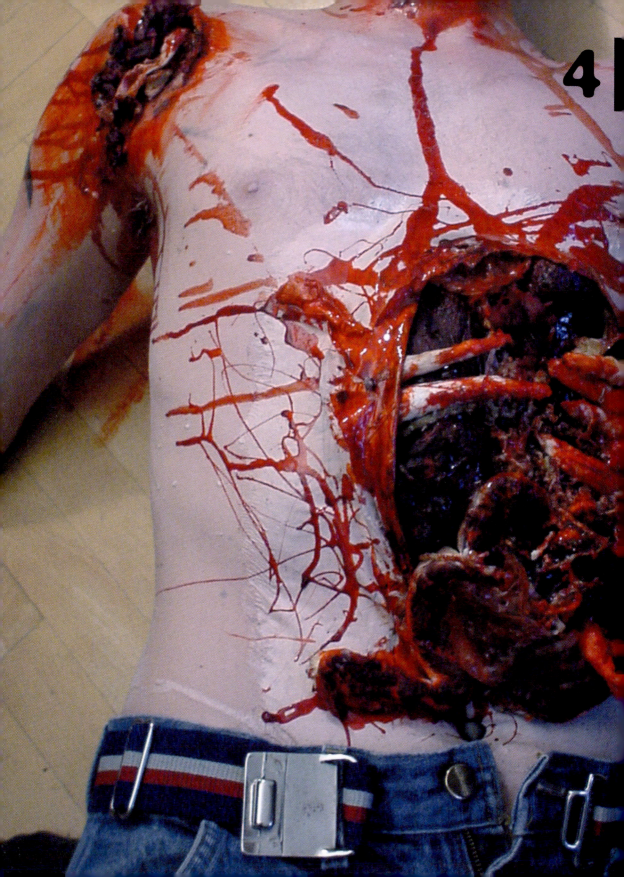

Shocking effects

These really violent effects are popular in the splatter-film genre, where the most extraordinary things happen. They can also be used by the fire brigade and ambulance service for practice drills; and of course for film, theatre and dramatic events.

Most of these effects require preparation, time and special materials. Some of the parts you can make yourself (see Chapter 2 on making artificial body parts, bones, eyes and entrails). It's a good idea to have a camera or video camera nearby, so you can document your effects when the work is done.

For these rather violent special effects, you have to make a whole arm, foot or leg out of latex, as well as pieces of latex skin (see the section on artificial body parts, page 28). The procedure for arms and legs is the same: for a blown-off arm, the actor holds their arm behind their back; for a blown-off leg, the leg is either bent out of sight or concealed in a hole in the ground. Place the blown- or cut-off body part at a short distance from the actor.

Materials:

Latex, talc or face powder, towels, an old saucepan, gelatine, water, glycerine, cotton wool or toilet paper, cream make-up (black, red, orange and skin-colours), bits of bone (chicken leftovers), blue cotton thread, theatrical blood, an artificial arm or leg.

Preparation

Making latex skin-pieces

Pour about a quarter of a cup of latex onto a plate of glass or other smooth surface. Spread out the latex so that it forms a pool the size of the skin on a leg. Imagine the skin of the lower half of a leg peeled and laid out flat on a tabletop: this is the size your pool of latex should be. Leave the latex to dry at room temperature, or dry it with a hairdryer. The latex turns a yellowish, translucent colour when it's dry. If there are still whitish blotches on the latex, it isn't completely dry. When the latex is thoroughly dry, powder it well with face powder or talc. When the latex is matt from the talc, it can be removed. Loosen part of the edge and pull off the whole piece of latex. Now powder the other side, to prevent it from sticking to itself, and your latex skin-piece is ready for use.

Concealing the real limb

Find the most effective way for the model to conceal their arm behind their back, or under their clothes. If you are modelling a cut-off leg, dig a hole in the ground about half a metre deep. (You can line the sides of the hole with towels to make it more comfortable for the actor.) Have the model stick their leg into the hole up to the knee, and fill in the hole with soil so it looks like the leg is missing from the knee down. (The actor should wear clothes which they don't mind getting dirty, or an appropriate costume if it's for a TV or theatre play.)

Preparation with latex/gelatine

Put two cups of powdered gelatine in an old saucepan. Add the same amount of water and bring to the boil, so you get a substance with the consistency of porridge. You can also just pour boiling water over the gelatine in a bowl. Add 1–2 tbsp glycerine to give the substance a more slimy consistency. Leave to cool until lukewarm. Dip pieces of cotton wool or toilet paper into the mixture; these will be used to simulate bits of flesh, sinews, and muscle tissue.

Alternatively, you can use liquid latex instead of gelatine. Dip cotton wool or toilet paper in the latex to model bits of flesh, sinews, and muscle tissue. It is also possible to combine the two materials.

Torn-off arm

Form a ring out of cotton wool and toilet paper around the shoulder, where the arm starts. Keep wetting the modelling material with gelatine mixture or liquid latex (see fig. 1). At the same time, build up little bits of flesh and sinews sticking out of the middle (see fig. 2). You can't avoid getting your hands very sticky, but try not to get gelatine or latex on hairy areas of the skin, by laying plastic over them. It is very important that the transition from the shoulder to the artificial continuation of the limb is smooth and even from the start. You won't be able to build out very far, as the weight will soon make the construction collapse; this doesn't present a problem, though, as we are simply modelling what's left of a blown-off or cut-off arm. To make the arm, place the latex skin-piece around some gelatine, either in one piece or in several smaller pieces. Place a few cotton threads under the skin: these will look like veins when viewed through the latex. In some areas, you should put a bit of gelatine mixture on the arm. When the work is finished, leave the gelatine to dry thoroughly. You can shorten the drying time by using a hairdryer.

Remember to supply the model with plenty of fluid, as, for obvious reasons, they won't be able to get this for themselves.

Now paint the gelatine with cream make-up. Use skin-colours near the real skin and reddish nuances where the skin is damaged and torn (see figs 3 and 4). Paint black and dark red where there are hollows and cavities in the wound to make them look deeper. Paint fleshy parts red and orange.

Fig. 1

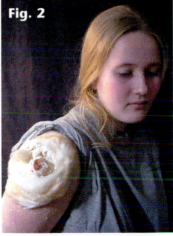

Fig. 2

Fig. 3

Fig. 4

Fig. 5

Let some sinewy bits remain the yellowish gelatine colour.

Now sprinkle theatrical blood over the area (see fig. 5). Consider where the veins run and how the accident happened. In which direction would the blood spurt, and how would the bleeding appear when the arm was torn or cut off?

Blown-off leg
Below is an alternative procedure for making a lost limb.

To give a more natural transition to the area where the limb is torn off, make an edge out of derma wax (see fig. 6). Smooth the edge

The right facial expression is important when the effect is to be filmed, photographed or seen by others.

towards the unscathed part of the leg and fray the derma wax towards the damaged part.

Now build up a ring to simulate the torn-off part, in the same way as described for the torn-off arm (see fig. 7). If you use gelatine, dry with cold air from a hairdryer. Hot air will prevent the gelatine from drying.

Paint the damaged part of the leg using cream make-up in reddish colours, and add plenty of blood. Place little pieces of gelatine and cotton wool smothered in blood, to resemble bits of flesh in the pool of blood (see figs 8 and 9).

If you have made an artificial leg, place it at an appropriate distance from the person and sprinkle blood on this too, making it look as if the parts belong together. If the model is wearing shoes, you must remember to put one shoe on the cut-off or blown-off leg. If someone noticed that the shoe was missing, the effect would be less convincing.

Removal

Gelatine is usually easy to remove from the skin, unless the area is hairy. Latex, on the other hand, sticks to both skin and hair, so you have to loosen the edges carefully – you can use washing-up liquid to help this process. Gelatine is a food product so leftovers cannot be kept, as they will slowly rot and go mouldy. If you have done the effect outside, don't leave leftovers in the garden where animals like foxes or birds may find them. Animals may suffocate if they eat gelatine which has been mixed with latex and cream make-up, so throw it in the bin. An artificial leg made of latex can of course be used again, but make sure that there is no gelatine left on it.

Student work done in class at the school
Enjoy Make-up.

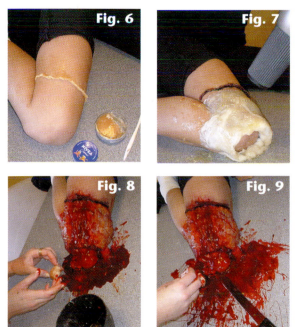

Fig. 6 · Fig. 7 · Fig. 8 · Fig. 9

This rather violent effect requires a few special materials and some well-coordinated acting.

Blown-out brains bald cap

Mount a ready-made bald cap on a glass or plastic bust (see page 64 for how to make a bald cap). Dip small pieces of cotton wool in a bowl of latex and, using a spatula, form a large crater on the bald cap where you want the brains to be blown out – as if by a shot from the opposite side. Fray the edges of the crater to imitate bits of skin and skull splinters, sticking out (see fig. 1). Apply several layers so you end up having a thick and durable blown-out brains bald cap (see fig. 2). In the bottom of the crater wound, model the actual hole in the skull randomly using strips and little bits of cotton wool and latex (see figs 3a and 3b).

Colouring

Now colour the bald cap with cream or rubber make-up in skin-colours. Colour right up to the flaps of skin at the back of the head (see figs 4a and 4b). Powder thoroughly to fix the colour on the latex.

Affixing the hair

Now you are going to put hair on the bald cap. You can use hair from a wig, wool crepe hair or any other kind of artificial hair (see the section on crepe hair and artificial beards, on page 60). Here you can see how to do it by cutting up an old wig (see fig. 5) and mounting it on the bald cap in pieces. If it's for the recording of a film, the colour and the style of the wig must match that of the actor's. Cut the wig into long strips which can easily be glued onto the bald cap. Apply a line of liquid latex to the bald cap and glue the wig strips into place one by one (see figs

Fig. 1

Fig. 2

Fig. 3a Fig. 3b

Fig. 4a

Fig. 4b

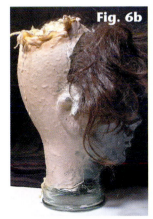

Fig. 6b

Fig. 6c

6a, 6b and 6c). Allow the latex to dry at regular intervals so the strips of wig aren't moved out of place. Little by little, the bald cap will get to look like a wig with a hole in the back of the head (see fig. 7). When finished, leave the product to dry thoroughly for a couple of hours.

Fig. 6a

Trim the strips of wig to fit the bald cap before mounting.

The blood tube

The rubber tube will transport blood from a syringe to the back of the head, and should be around 0.5 cm in diameter. You can get these from pet shops that sell aquarium equipment, or from a hospital or emergency ward (see fig. 8). Preferably, the tube should be at least a metre long as it will run out of

Fig. 7

Fig. 5

Wig hair is usually mounted in lines, which makes it easy to cut into strips.

Fig. 8

sight, concealed under the clothes. Seal one end of the tube by melting it with a lighter. With a sharp knife, make a few holes, about 0.5 cm apart, in the closed end of the tube. Make the holes about 2–3 mm in diameter. Affix the other end of the tube to a syringe, which you can fill with theatrical blood.

Affixing the rubber tube

With a knife or a pair of scissors, make one or several holes in the middle of the crater. Mount the tube on the inside of the bald cap with the holes placed so that they open into the hole in the bald cap. Affix the tube with gaff tape or something similar (see fig. 9). Seal the area of the hole in the cap and holes in the tube with cotton wool and latex, but be careful that latex doesn't run into the holes in the tube and block them. Let the latex seal dry completely before testing by squirting water through the tube and holes (see fig. 10).

Concealing the holes

The blood holes are still clearly visible on the outside and must be concealed with a bit of latex fluff. This is the bits of dry latex you often find on the inside of the lid or rub off your fingers when working with latex. The fluff quite closely resembles bits of skin and flesh when painted. Place a little fluff over the holes so it looks like bits of skin, but don't cover the holes completely or the blood won't be able to spurt out. When you've put the latex fluff on, you can pour a bit of liquid latex over the area to keep the fluff in place (see fig. 11). Avoid getting liquid latex in the holes or you will block them. Again, the latex must be allowed to dry completely before you continue. Now colour

the actual back of the head with cream make-up in red and black tones, and with theatrical blood. The blown-out brains bald cap is now ready for use.

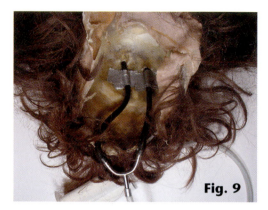

Fig. 9

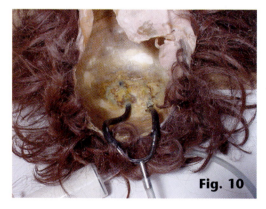

Fig. 10

Fig. 11

Mounting the bald cap and tube

Mount the bald-cap wig and glue it in place in the same way as an ordinary bald cap (see page 66). If the cap is only to be worn for a short time and the actor isn't going to be moving about, you can simply put on the bald cap just as you would an ordinary wig. Conceal the hose, which runs from the inside of the bald cap, under the clothes; it has to run beneath the collar and shirt and out at the bottom of the shirt. The tube must be long enough for the make-up artist to operate the syringe filled with theatrical blood, out of sight of the camera.

When you've filled the syringe with blood, lightly press in the piston so that blood runs into the tube. The idea is that the blood runs all the way through the tube until it is 10–15 cm from the opening. The reason for this is that, at the right moment, you want all the

blood to spurt out in one go, as soon as the syringe is emptied. It may be necessary to fill the syringe again after you have injected blood into the hose. This cannot be done by pulling back the piston, as doing this will simply suck the blood back into the syringe again. You have to temporarily take the syringe off the hose, hold your finger over the end of the hose so the blood doesn't run out while you refill the syringe with blood, then put the syringe and hose back together again.

When the actor is shot and is pushed back by the impact, the blood is supposed to spurt out of the back of the head when the make-up artist empties the syringe. It is important to hold onto both syringe and tube, otherwise the tube may come off the syringe and the blood end up in the wrong place. Always use blood that can be washed off so that the bald cap, hair and anything else can be washed clean afterwards.

Ready for shooting: fill the syringe with blood, dress up the actor and cover up the walls and floor.

Affix the blood tube underneath the clothes using sticky tape.

Angle of fire.

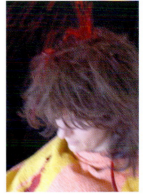

This effect requires thorough planning. Consider where the stomach is to be cut open, and find out which entrails will be visible in the chosen place.

Materials:

A rubber tube, a syringe (the kind with no needle), a sharp knife, a lighter, a glass or plastic bust, cotton wool, latex, a small bowl, spatula, bald cap, scissors, gaff tape, a wig or crepe hair, various make-up colours, theatrical blood.

The following are optional: Cernit, rubber tube and a syringe.

Fig. 1

The effect lends itself best to recordings where the victim is relatively still, and for photographs. The reason is that entrails, slime and blood easily fall out if the victim is moving about.

The whole stomach cut open

Cover the floor with plastic to prevent it from getting covered in blood and gelatine. Have the model lie comfortably on the floor on their back.

Fig. 2

Place a piece of cling film or clear carrier-bag plastic on the middle of the stomach or chest, so there is at least 3 cm of bare skin around the plastic. Lay the film double, thereby creating a pocket (see fig. 1). Apply latex to the film and stomach so that the 3 cm of bare skin is also covered. Dry the latex with a hairdryer and apply several more layers of latex – 4–5 layers altogether. Allow to dry thoroughly (see figs 2 and 3).

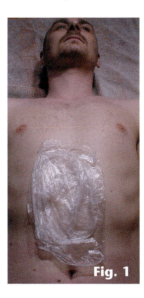
Fig. 3

Now powder the stomach with talc or face powder (see fig. 4). Carefully lift the artificial stomach skin and make a small hole in the middle using the spatula. Cut a slit from the hole in the latex skin, but don't go closer to the edge than 3–4 cm (see figs 5 and 6). Now expand the hole into a small pocket with a spatula or your fingers. Be careful you don't get too close to the edge and ruin the pocket. This pocket will hold entrails, blood, bones and tissue (see fig. 7). If possible, remove the film or plastic which was put on in the beginning to create the pocket effect. If the latex makes this difficult, it's better to leave the plastic on; otherwise you risk tearing the latex skin (see fig. 8).

Fig. 6

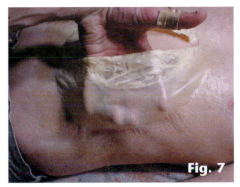
Fig. 7

Fig. 4

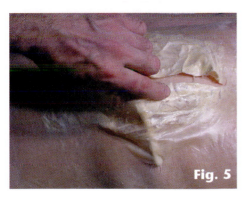
Fig. 5

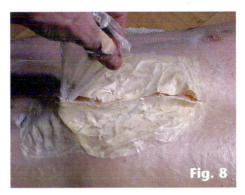
Fig. 8

Pull the flaps of skin a little to one side and paint the bottom of the hole in black, dark red and reddish tones. Make a couple of cylinders out of cotton wool and carefully place these inside the stomach pocket. When the cotton wool is inside the pocket, push it

towards the sides, opening the pocket a little
(see fig. 9). Be careful not to make the bulge
too high as this will make the effect
unrealistic.

Paint the outside of the stomach skin-
coloured using foundation, cream or water-
based make-up. Then powder lightly with
face powder or talc to give the skin a more
matt appearance. Fold back the latex
stomach flaps a little, and paint the inside of
the stomach-skin red with cream make-up or
theatrical blood (see fig. 10).

Now push a little latex in between the
entrails to resemble sinews, muscles and
tissue. Use a spatula to push it into place (see
fig. 11). Arrange the modelled entrails in
relation to each other, possibly so that they
fall out of the stomach when it is cut open –
but stick to the correct anatomical
positioning. You can't avoid the stomach
looking a little larger than an actual stomach
is; after all, there has to be room for an extra
set of entrails (see fig. 12). Add a little
theatrical blood and blood paste, which is
slightly thicker than theatrical blood,
between the entrails (see fig. 13).

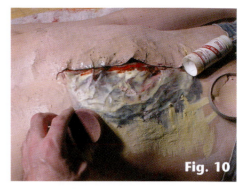

Fig. 10

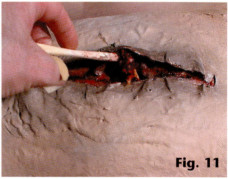

Fig. 11

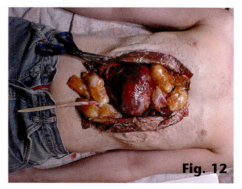

Fig. 12

Fig. 9

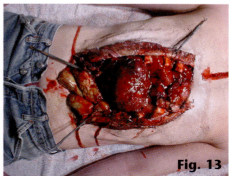

Fig. 13

You can now colour the entrails. Use water-based make-up, cream make-up or another kind of liquid or cream-based make-up. Look in an encyclopaedia of anatomy or a medical book, to see which colour the chosen entrails are. After a brutal cutting open of the stomach there will be lots of blood, as many veins will have been torn open. Many of the entrails are an orangey-red to dark-red colour (see fig. 14). Paint the liver dark red, bordering on bordeaux if it's a healthy liver (see fig. 15). Paint the bowels yellow-green to turquoise and brown, depending on the state of the bowels (see fig. 16). When all the entrails have been painted, give them a coat of lacquer to make them shiny.

Now apply a thin layer of Vaseline, rich clear lotion or glycerine to the entrails, or add a little clear liquid soap to simulate tissue fat and slime. These final touches can really make it look horrible (see fig. 17). You can also pull the flaps of skin together a bit. Sprinkle theatrical blood over the wound.

Note: If the actual chest is ripped open, you will be able to see the ribs and lungs. Rib bones can be made out of Cernit or strips of cotton wool soaked in latex. If you want it to look like the victim has been dead for some time, the face and arms must be given the corpse make-up treatment (see page 74).

The ripped-open stomach effect is a once-only prop, as the whole thing will come to pieces when you remove it. Furthermore, if you have used gelatine, this will go mouldy in a couple of weeks as it is a food product.

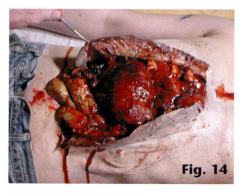

Fig. 14

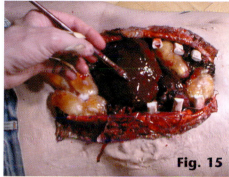

Fig. 15

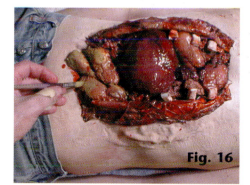

Fig. 16

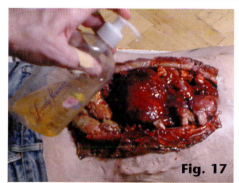

Fig. 17

Creative ideas

If you want blood to spurt out of the ripped-open stomach, lay a rubber tube under the artificial stomach-skin, after the entrails have been put in. Make a hole for the tube in one side of the skin of the stomach, making sure the opening of the tube isn't blocked and that it is hidden from view. Affix a syringe filled with theatrical blood to the other end of the tube. Pump rhythmically to simulate the heart pumping out blood.

If you want to show the heart still beating, you can place a little toy jumping frog underneath the heart and entrails. (You can buy a kind of toy frog which has a tube and an air pump attached to it, which makes it jump.)

Another ripped-open stomach, modelled by students on a weekend course that I tutored. Here the victim has also had his throat and shoulder cut, and you can see a couple of the ribs.

After splatter-work, there's always plenty of cleaning up to do. You would almost think a mass murderer had been at work!

A zombie pulls a girl by the hair through a broken door full of splinters and her eye is pierced by a wooden splinter. A scientist raises a rifle to shoot a madman; the bullet hits him directly in the eye. A girl defends herself against a psychotic murderer, by poking his eyes out with a knitting needle.

Two methods of creating these effects are described here: one where only the eye has been ripped out, and one where the face has also been smashed.

Gouged eye

Materials:
Toilet paper or cotton wool, scissors, derma wax, rich moisturiser, spatula, cream make-up (red, black, skin-coloured) and theatrical blood.

Soften a piece of derma wax and roll it into a cylinder. Mount the cylinder over the globe line (the little fold in the skin above the eyelid). Tone the wax upwards towards the brow using a little rich moisturiser, creating a smooth transition to the skin. Soften another piece of derma wax and place it directly below the eye. Tone downwards in the same way as described above (see fig. 1).

Cut out a small semi-circle, the size of the eyelid, from a cotton pad or some toilet paper, and moisten with water. Place the semi-circle on the eye while it is closed, so that it covers the entire area inside the derma-wax border (see fig. 2). Paint the eye socket with black cream make-up and with reddish tones around the edge of the eye socket, both on the inside and outside of the wax. You can also add a little face cream, for instance Nivea, to the cream make-up, if you

have difficulty painting on the cotton wool with it (see fig. 3). Outside the wax ring, tone towards the skin, using a little skin-coloured and reddish cream make-up or foundation. Now pour a little theatrical blood into the eye hollow (see fig. 4).

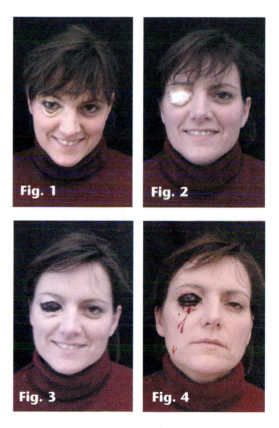

Fig. 1

Fig. 2

Fig. 3

Fig. 4

If you want it to look like the eye has been smashed, tear a bit of toilet paper into shreds. Dip it in theatrical blood and place it in the eye socket. Let a little theatrical blood run down the cheek from the eye socket (see figs 5 and 6).

Fig. 5 Fig. 6

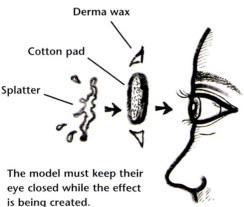

Derma wax

Cotton pad

Splatter

The model must keep their eye closed while the effect is being created.

Gouged eye with smashed face

Materials:
Powdered gelatine, boiling water in a bowl, glycerine, mixing stick, cotton wool pads, spatula, cotton wool, derma wax, rich moisturiser, artificial eye, hairdryer, cream or water-based make-up (red, black, blue, yellow), theatrical blood, latex (optional).

Mix 3 tbsp of powdered gelatine with boiling water in a bowl. Add 1 tbsp of glycerine and mix it together until you get a consistency like porridge.

Soften a piece of derma wax and roll it into several cylinders. Mount one cylinder around the eye like a ring, corresponding to the area where the skin has been ripped open. Start the ring a little above the eye and let it go a little down onto the cheek. Tone the wax edges using a little rich moisturiser, so you get a smooth transition (see fig. 1).

Cover the model's eye and eyebrow with cotton pads, within the area of the derma wax (see fig. 2). Using a spatula or spoon, apply a little lukewarm gelatine mixture to the cotton wool in the derma-wax circle (or, if you haven't used derma wax, around the cotton pads on the eye, to make the cotton wool stick to the skin). Slowly cover the whole area with gelatine mixture, so it looks like brain tissue has been squeezed out of the eye socket.

Form a little fold or pocket in the gelatine for the gouged eye, and insert the artificial eye (see fig. 3). (Be sure to use an eye of the same colour as the model's.) You can also form a thick thread out of gelatine to simulate the optic nerve, running from the eye socket to the gouged eye. Now let the gelatine mask dry: this will take about 10 minutes. You can shorten the drying time by using a hairdryer. Use cold air, as warm air will prevent the gelatine from drying completely.

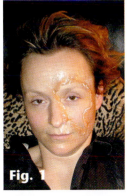

Fig. 1

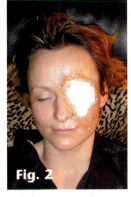

Fig. 2

You can now paint the mask with cream or water-based make-up: dark reddish shades in the deepest areas, bluish tones on sinewy parts, and blood colours on the rest of the wound. Don't forget to add a general reddening of the surrounding, unscathed skin (see fig. 4). If you like, apply a little theatrical blood running down the cheeks and on the artificial eye. Add theatrical blood all round to make the effect more dramatic (see fig. 5).

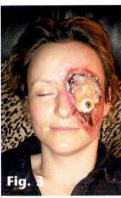

Fig. 3

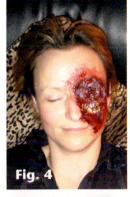

Fig. 4

You could also let the eye hang loosely from the optic nerve. Roll a little hardened latex into a long thread and affix it to the artificial eye. Colour the thread using red cream make-up or theatrical blood. Affix the other end of the optic nerve to the eye socket using gelatine mixture or a little latex. Don't make the optic nerve too long.

Fig. 5

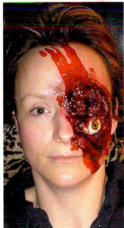

Instead of using gelatine, you can use latex and cotton wool alone for this effect. Note, however, that latex may make the eyes water if it gets too close to them.

If a broken bone doesn't break the skin, the fracture is termed a 'closed fracture'. If, on the other hand, bits of bone stick out, and skin and soft tissue is damaged, you call it an 'open fracture'.

A 'displaced' or 'angled' fracture means that two fractured parts have moved away from their normal anatomical position. In the case of a fracture, there is always a certain amount of damage to the surrounding tissue. Blood vessels and nerves may be damaged and the skin will be discoloured and bruised.

The term 'fracture' covers everything from minor surface cracks to clean breaks through the whole bone.

Closed fracture

Materials:
Derma wax, spatula, cream make-up (blue, red), brushes or a sponge, face powder.

Soften a piece of derma wax and spread it onto the skin where you want the fracture to be, so it looks like a small swelling. Smooth the transition from wax to skin. Press the palm of your hand into the wax, leaving an impression of the skin in the wax.

Leave the swollen part the yellow derma-wax colour. Around the swelling, tone with blue-red shades, to make a bruise at the stage of your choice. Powder the swelling lightly.

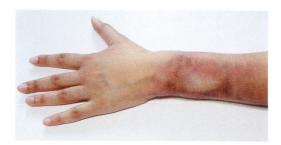

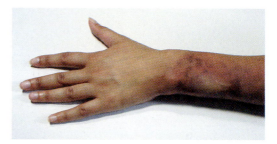

Closed fracture in various stages.

Open fracture

Materials:
Derma wax, spatula, animal bones or artificial bone pieces made of Cernit, cream make-up (blue, red), theatrical blood.

For this effect you need bone splinters, which must be small, oblong and wedge-shaped. Place a softened piece of derma wax on the skin as a bump. The size of the derma-wax piece can be anything from the size of a pea to that of a half walnut. Smooth the edge of the wax using a spatula and make sure that the swelling isn't unnaturally high (see fig. 1). Make a groove in the middle and stick one or more bone splinters into the groove. Place the splinters at different angles, so it looks like a real fracture (see figs 2a, 2b and 2c). Use cream make-up colour in bluish and reddish tones around the swollen area, but leave the bump itself pale and skin-coloured (see figs 3a, 3b and 3c). Pour theatrical blood into the actual wound and sprinkle a couple of drops around the bone splinters (see figs 4a and 4b).

Fig. 1

Fig. 2a

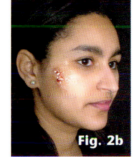

Fig. 2b

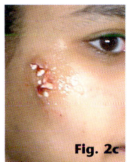

Fig. 2c

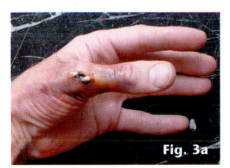

Fig. 3a

Fig. 3b

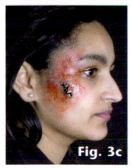

Fig. 3c

Fig. 4a

Fig. 4b

Severe fracture
Method 1

Materials:
Derma wax, rich moisturiser, spatula, face powder or talc, cream make-up (black, red, dark red, blue), theatrical blood, fresh scratch and a specially made piece of bone.

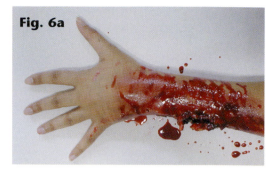

Fig. 6a

Place an appropriately sized piece of derma wax on the skin to simulate a swelling. Smooth the edges of the wax with a spatula and make sure that the swelling isn't unnaturally high. Make a groove in the middle and stick the specially designed bone piece into the groove. The skin should be ripped open where the bone is supposed to have broken through. Colour the base of the wound with black cream make-up and around the swollen area in bluish and reddish tones, but leave the actual swelling pale and skin-coloured (see fig. 5).

Add fresh scratch and theatrical blood to the wound, and sprinkle blood onto the arm around the wound, depending on how gory you want the effect to be (see figs 6a, 6b and 6c).

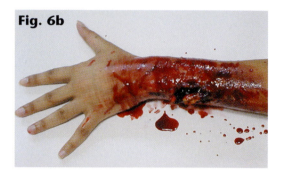

Fig. 6b

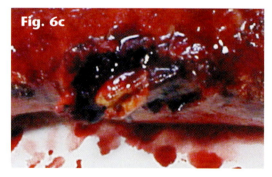

Fig. 6c

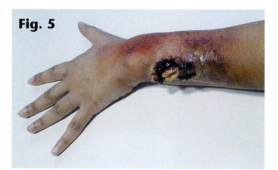

Fig. 5

Skin

Flat-bottomed piece of bone (see the section on artificial bones, page 31).

Method 2

Materials:

Gelatine powder, bowl, boiling water, mixing stick, spatula, glycerine, mincemeat and bristle (optional), hairdryer, cream make-up (black, red, blue), theatrical blood and a specially designed piece of bone.

Mix 3 tbsp of powdered gelatine with boiling water in a bowl. Add 1 tbsp of glycerine and mix to the consistency of porridge. Affix the specially made bone piece to the leg or arm. Place thin strips of cotton wool soaked in the gelatine around the bone so that only the broken end is visible. Note that even though the bone is supposed to be broken, it still has to run parallel to the rest of the bone. Conceal the transition from gelatine to skin by smoothing with a spatula. Push a little of the gelatine in between the pieces of bone, to simulate flesh and sinews. Alternatively, use real mincemeat with bristle. Dry the gelatine with cold air from a hairdryer.

Colour the wound using black and dark red cream make-up for the base of the wound. Around the wound, tone with blue and reddish shades some way onto the real skin. Pour blood in and around the wound.

Suggestion:
You can also make a piece of artificial skin by pouring a little liquid latex onto a glass plate, creating a little pool of approximately 10 x 10 cm. Dry thoroughly with a hairdryer, until the latex is almost translucent. Powder the latex patch with talc or face powder and carefully peel it off. Also powder the reverse side. Press this piece of latex skin into the derma wax so that it covers part of the bones and flesh. Then push it back a little, so it looks like skin that has been pushed back during the fracturing of the bone. Sprinkle a little blood over it.

When you see fire and explosions on film, you are seeing the work of pyro-technicians. 'Pyro-' is derived from the Greek word 'pyros', which means fire. This section deals with suppurating burns from accidents involving fire and explosions.

When you burn yourself, the skin and underlying tissue are damaged; the area around the burns may also be damaged. Tissue fluid cannot be retrieved through the veins, causing infiltration of fluid, starting at the burned area and spreading to and around the burn.

Burns can be made up in various ways, using different materials and ingredients. Therefore, it is important to decide which kind of effect you want to create and to know how the different ingredients look and work. There is no list of materials in this chapter, as burns can be done in so many different ways.

Clinically, burns are divided into three categories (in Europe):

First degree: Involves the epidermis (the top layer of skin) but not the lower layers – the basal cell layer, where cell regeneration takes place. There is reddening of the skin and sensitivity is maintained.

Second degree: Also involves the basal cell layer in the epidermis. In deep second-degree burns, hair follicles and sweat glands are also affected. There is suppuration (blisters), reddening of the skin and build-up of fluid, due to the accumulation of lymph fluid. Sensitivity is maintained.

Third degree: The burn affects the deeper-lying tissue. Sweat glands, hair follicles, vessels and nerves are destroyed. The burned area may be black and charred if the burn was caused by a naked flame, and whitish or a deep red if caused by scalding. In the periphery of the burned area, there is often a broad area of red skin because of dilated blood vessels. There is no feeling in the skin.

In the case of burns covering large areas of the body, the burned area is assessed according to the '9% rule'; for instance, a whole arm constitutes 9% of the surface of the body; a whole leg 18%; the front or back of the torso 18%; the head and neck 9%; and the hand and all five fingers, constitute 1%.

First degree burn
UV radiation or scalding by water

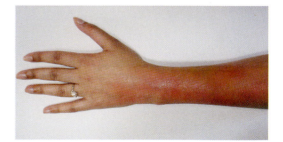

This effect is easy to do. You can use cream make-up or eye shadow in orange and red colours. Tint the area you want to look burned. Avoid sharp edges and abrupt transitions from the tinted area to the natural skin.

In burns that are more than 4–5 days old, there is coagulated lymph fluid around the burn. From second degree burns upwards, the burn always suppurates a lot, as lymph fluid collects around the burn to protect the wound. Lymph, which is a clear fluid, can be simulated with glycerine. Coagulated lymph, however, can be yellow ochre to olive green in colour. The reason for this is that dust and dirt accumulate in the wound. If the coagulated lymph is mixed with coagulated blood, it is a more brownish colour. You can make up coagulated lymph using Tuplast, coloured with cream make-up.

Peeling skin

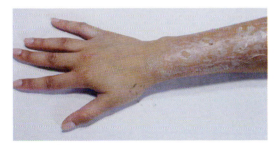

Apply a layer of latex to the skin and let it dry. Use a hairdryer to save time. Rip up the surface of the latex slightly using the pointed end of a spatula; this will make it look like the skin is peeling. You can also rub the surface of the latex, to make it resemble skin flaking after too much sun.

Burns with blisters

These are caused by hot surfaces such as a hotplate, or contact with molten metal.

Squeeze some Tuplast directly onto the skin. Shape the Tuplast so it looks like little blisters. Carefully rub on a little glycerine (see fig. 1). You have now modelled the first stages of burn blisters.

If you want to model a deeper burn where more of the skin is damaged, squeeze out a little more Tuplast. Press some of it onto the skin and shape it into a hollow in the skin. Colour the affected area with reddish-orange cream make-up and blend it well into the surrounding area (see figs 2 and 3). The colour depends to a certain extent on how severe the burn is. Burns always suppurate heavily because of lymph fluid rushing to the wound. For this reason, you should never powder make-up burns: rather you should add to the wet look by applying glycerine, for

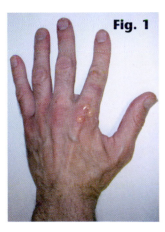

Fig. 1

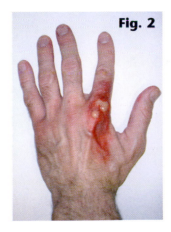

Fig. 2

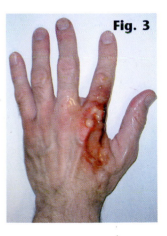

Fig. 3

instance. Burns are generally a red, orange or yellow colour.

If the skin has come off so the wound opens into the blood stream, add theatrical blood to the wound. The burn will still suppurate, but the lymph fluid will be mixed with blood (see fig. 4). If you want a very severe-looking burn, pour a little yellow liquid soap in the wound. Mixed with theatrical blood, this will look like pus coming from the burn.

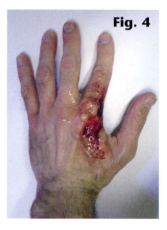

Fig. 4

Second degree burn
Extreme UV radiation or severe scalding from boiling water
This effect can be done as a continuation of the peeling-skin effect. Latex has been applied onto the skin, dried with a hairdryer and ripped up to simulate areas of broken skin. Where the skin is broken, paint with reddish and pinkish colours to represent the lower layers of skin. Tint a little darker around the edges, and orangey-yellow on the surrounding skin. Add some glycerine with a sponge to make the skin shiny.

It is essential to blend the colours on the actual burn gradually into the colour of the surrounding skin.

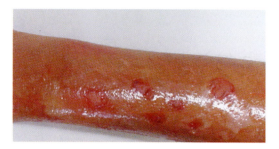

Third degree burn
Contact with red-hot metal or any other extremely hot material
You can either use liquid latex or a gelatine mixture for this effect. If you work with gelatine, this has to be mixed beforehand:

Mix 3 tbsp of gelatine powder and 1 tbsp of glycerine with boiling water. Mix it to a porridge-like consistency. Stir in a couple of strips of cotton wool, and leave to cool until lukewarm. Now your gelatine mix is ready.

If you decide to work with latex, pour a little latex into a bowl and add a couple of cotton wool strips.

Start by tinting the skin reddish and orange with cream make-up or eye shadow, to get a base colour. Now apply latex or gelatine to the skin. Blend the edges into the surrounding area, so you get a smooth transition. Shape a wound with walls around it, to make it look like the skin has recoiled from the extreme heat (see fig. 5). At this stage, the effect could pass as a deep second degree burn in the first stage. Colour the inner wall of the mounds sufficiently dark to create an illusion of depth. Leave the edges uncoloured, or colour them whitish and yellowish (see fig. 6). Apply theatrical blood and glycerine to the base of the wound (see figs 7, 8 and 9). Tint around the mounds and towards the unscathed skin with red, brown, black and yellow cream make-up.

Make the entire burn area look wet by applying a layer of glycerine. You can also apply a little Vaseline to the edges of the wound, which will look like coagulated lymph or pus. Sprinkle on some theatrical blood (see fig. 10).

Here, the wound is shown with maggots eating the dead tissue, to make the effect look extra horrible (see fig. 11). The maggots are in fact edible, as they are actually crisps, which you can buy in practical joke shops.

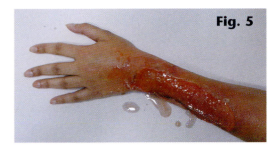
Fig. 5

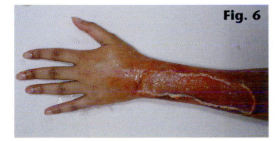
Fig. 6

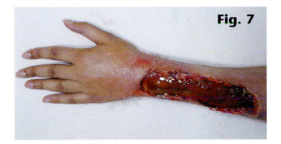
Fig. 7

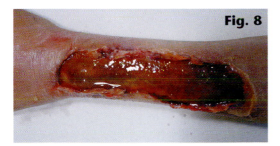
Fig. 8

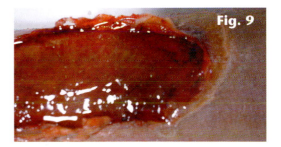
Fig. 9

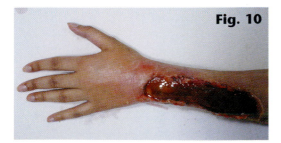
Fig. 10

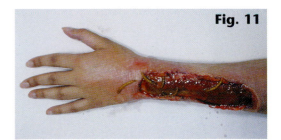
Fig. 11

Charred burn – contact with open fire and flames or an explosion

Charring may be caused by burning from flames, and the skin and flesh may be literally fried, in a manner similar to a steak being burned on a frying pan. In connection with extreme heat, there may be superficial formation of ash. In the case of a naked flame, there will also be soot, for example, from burning wood, passed on from sooty smoke, and the clothes may be scorched.

Add extra black colour to the wound, by carefully dabbing on black cream make-up, especially on scabs around edges of the wound. You can use a bristle sponge for this. You can also sprinkle ashes onto the burn: use cigarette ash, or ash from a burned cork or something similar. Black eye shadow can also be used. Scrape a little powder off the surface of the eye shadow and sprinkle it over the burn.

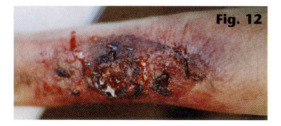

Fig. 12

The skin is deformed and wrinkles easily – extreme radiation or contact with red-hot surfaces

Soften a couple of balls of derma wax. Place them on the skin and shape them into blisters. Smooth the edges to conceal the transition from wax to skin, but be careful not to flatten the tops of the wax mounds; these must remain high and round. Tint the area around the blisters red with cream make-up. You can't use red eye shadow for this, because it will clot easily in the slightly greasy derma wax (see fig. 13).

Apply latex to the area around the blisters. Place small pieces of toilet paper over the wet latex (divide the toilet paper into single layers to get as thin a layer of paper as possible). Do not cover the actual wax blisters with either latex or paper. If necessary, you can apply a little extra latex on top of the paper. Crumple the paper slightly to make it look like wrinkled skin (see fig. 14). Leave it to dry. Make a couple of little holes in the latex skin to simulate patches of damaged skin.

The latex must be completely dry before you paint on it with a brush – otherwise, the brush may be ruined. Paint the wrinkled skin in brown, reddish, yellow and black colours, darkest around the little holes, and a pale red in the bottom of wounds to simulate the sub-cutis (lower layers of skin). Tint a little reddish make-up around the entire burn area and blend into the surrounding skin (see figs 15 and 16).

Drip a little glycerine over the wound to simulate lymph fluid, and finish off by sprinkling a bit of black ash and some theatrical blood over the wound (see fig. 17).

Electric burn – contact with high voltage cables or stricken by lightning

If a person gets a high voltage electric shock, the skin may be scorched and burned black by heat and sparks from the charge.

Soften a piece of derma wax the size of a hazelnut. Squash it flat on the skin and

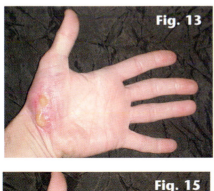

Fig. 13

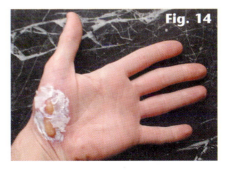

Fig. 14

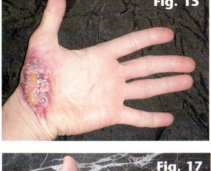

Fig. 15

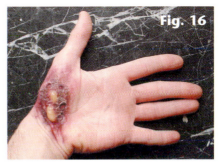

Fig. 16

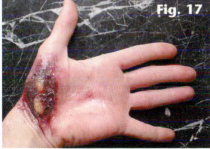

Fig. 17

but not as much as for a bloody cut or wound.

Tint lightly around the hollows with reddish shades (see fig. 19). Powder the wound well to give it a matt appearance.

Now, give the skin surrounding the wound a pale and anaemic appearance, using cream make-up or camouflage make-up in light skin-colours. Blend the colour into the reddish tones around the hollows to get a natural look. Powder again (see fig. 20).

Scabs after scorching – formation of scabs a couple of days after a severe burn

Apply latex to the burned area. Sprinkle porridge oats onto the wet latex; later, this will become scabs and flakes of skin (see fig. 21). For a larger area of severe burning, cornflakes can be used instead. Apply a little latex on top

flatten until it appears merely as a swollen area of skin. If the wax is too hard, add a little rich moisturiser to soften it.

Scrape hollows in the wax using a spatula, to make it look like the skin has been scorched off in a way similar to how a plastic bag melts when it burns (see fig. 18).

Paint with cream make-up in black and brownish tones in the hollow of the wound. Drip a little theatrical blood into the wound, of the oats or cornflakes to keep them in place and dry with a hairdryer (see fig. 22).

When the latex is dry, paint the scabs in brownish, yellowish and reddish tones. If the transition to the actual skin is too abrupt, then apply a thin layer of Kleenex or single-layer toilet paper dipped in latex. Shape the periphery of the wound to look like skin that has wrinkled because of the burning (see fig. 23).

Colour the edges of each scab black or dark brown with cream make-up. Then colour the actual wound using orange, reddish and brownish tones. Remember to blend the colour gradually into the surrounding skin, to get a realistic look (see fig. 24).

As the wound isn't completely fresh, it doesn't have to suppurate all that heavily: powder the wound lightly with translucent face powder or talc. However, if you want the wound to look like it hasn't healed yet, add a little Vaseline to simulate pus. If scabs and flakes of skin have loosened, causing light bleeding, dab gently with pale red theatrical blood (see fig. 25).

Real photos

On the opposite page is a photo series of a mild second degree burn during the course of a year, up until total healing.

To become really good at making up realistic burns, you must study pictures of actual ones. You can find such pictures in medical books, on the Internet and in magazines.

This photo series shows a burn that I got while casting stunt bottles. Stunt bottles look like real glass bottles, but you can break them over someone's head without causing injury; they are made by pouring a special liquid plastic alloy into silicone moulds. Unfortunately, I got some hot plastic on my hand and, although I quickly got the plastic

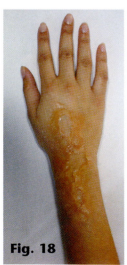

Fig. 18

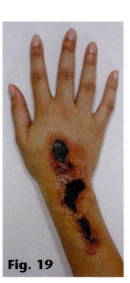

Fig. 19

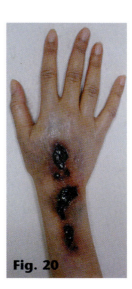

Fig. 20

Fig. 21

Fig. 22

Fig. 23

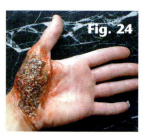

Fig. 24

Fig. 25

off my hand and held it under cold water, I was left with a large blister where the epidermis had been scorched off. It was very painful of course, but I thought that I had better photograph it while I had the chance.

I photographed the burn regularly to document the various stages. However, as different cameras were used and under different circumstances, the quality varies quite a bit. You still get an idea of the closing of the wound, scab formation and formation of new skin, though.

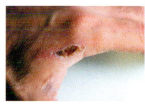

After 10 days: the wound no longer suppurates; slight scab formation.

After approximately 3 weeks: ordinary scab.

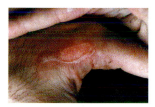

Photographed half an hour after the accident: a blister has appeared and a part of the skin has been scorched off.

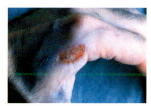

After a little over a month: new skin where the blister was; dry scab.

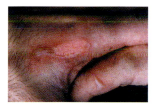

The following day: there is also a small blister on the adjoining finger.

After a couple of months: new skin has formed, which is still pink.

After 5 days: pieces of dead skin have fallen off; the wound still suppurates.

After about a year: the wound has healed completely; the scar is barely visible.

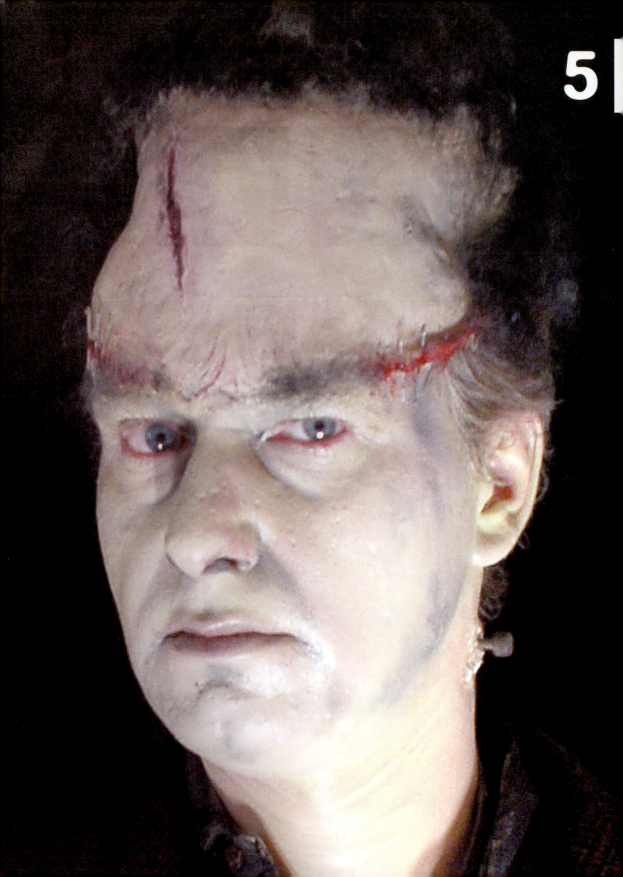

Classic monsters & creatures

This chapter deals with some of the best-known monsters and scary characters in the history of film and theatre. The methods for creating these monsters will be explained step by step, but there are both easy and more difficult ways of creating each monster. The make-up for Darth Maul described here, for instance, is pretty easy to do, while more difficult methods have been chosen for Frankenstein's monster and Pinhead. Accordingly, I have taken the liberty of interpreting the characters, not only according to my personal taste, but also taking into consideration the limitations and advantages of each method. Having done this, I urge the reader to choose the method you believe is best suited to each particular monster.

In addition to make-up and the making of masks, there are suggestions for costumes and special props, which help to make the character come to life. There is even a little history and background information for each character, so you get an idea of what you're working on and why they look the way they do. In most cases, titles of films and videos for each monster are mentioned, in case you should want to do some research or see the real thing.

The best-known monster is the vampire, which can be found in countless myths and tales from all over the world. A vampire is a so-called 'undead', which to exist needs to drink the blood of the living.

Vlad the Impaler (1431–1476), better known as the historical Dracula, is said to have been a cunning sadist who took pleasure in large scale mass murder.

The name Dracula originates from the Rumanian word Drac, which means devil or dragon. During the war against the Huns, Vlad executed about 500 Rumanian Bojars by having them impaled them on sharpened wooden poles, to avenge the death of his father. He believed that one of them was his father's murderer and so killed them all. However, in Rumania, of which Transylvania is a part, Dracula is looked upon as a national hero, as he fought for his country and a holy cause by striving to drive the Turks out of Central Europe. In 1978, the writer Nicolae Romaniae attempted to erase the negative image of Dracula in his book *Bibliotheca Historica Romanie*, but without much success: the myth of Dracula is as alive as ever.

In 1897, Bram Stoker wrote his famous novel *Dracula*, inspired by the story of Vlad Tepes Dracula. The story was made into a film as early as 1922, by the film-maker F. W. Murnau. Due to copyright problems, however, it was released under the title *Nosferatu* and the character of Count Dracula was called Count Orlok. Since then, the book has inspired countless films, theatre productions and books, creating the mythical Dracula character we now know so well, along with a special set of rules applying to vampires: Dracula can take on the form of a bat, a dog or a rat, and he can evaporate into fog. He can also communicate with wolves, rats, snakes and bats. In addition to this, Dracula has supernatural strength, and he lives off the blood of humans, preferably that of beautiful young women. In many films, he is portrayed as an irresistible and seductive 'Prince Charming'. This contrasts with other vampires, which are often portrayed as repulsive and horrific. Several things are harmful, even deadly to Dracula: crosses, holy water, mirrors, sunlight and the smell of garlic. He can only sleep in a coffin full of soil from his homeland. Dracula can only be destroyed if a wooden stake is driven through his heart, or his head is separated from his body.

Four different methods for creating a vampire, on different levels of difficulty, are described below:

1) The well-dressed Dracula
(Inspired by the film *Dracula* (1931) starring Bela Lugosi. Use: films, theatre and parties.)

2) The dramatic vampire
(Main use: films and photos.)

3) Children's painted Dracula
(Use: primarily fancy dress parties and events for children.)

The well-dressed Dracula

Materials:
Brushes and sponges, light foundation or white cake make-up, cream make-up (yellow, white, black, blue, dark red), eye shadow (greyish-brown), red eye pencil, theatrical blood, vampire teeth, black hairspray or water-based make-up.

The following are optional: hair gel, Dracula costume, etc.

Make up the face, hands and neck a pallid colour with a very light foundation, white cake make-up or yellowish cream make-up. Use a make-up sponge and be careful not to turn the face of the model too white; you don't want him to look like Pierrot.

Draw eyebrows using black cream make-up. Apply dark greyish-brown eye shadow below the cheekbones and along the nose. Tint a dark shadow around the inner corners of the eye and onto the eyelids, to make the eyes look deep-set and scary. To create a frowning expression, tint two vertical shadows between the eyebrows using a thin brush. Colour the wet ridge of the lower eyelid, or the area directly below the lower lashes, blood red using a red eye pencil or red cream make-up. You can also use theatrical blood. Tint the lips a bluish colour with cream make-up. If the vampire has just eaten, colour the mouth blood red with cream make-up and theatrical blood.

Make the vampire wear a set of fangs, either a ready-made set or your own homemade fangs (see the section on making false teeth on page 34). Then colour the hair black with black water-based make-up (which you can wash out). If necessary, use gel to flatten the hair.

Dracula is a very classy dresser and typically wears a tuxedo and a cloak. He also sometimes wears a black or dark-grey high hat and white gloves.

The dramatic vampire

Materials:
Brushes and sponges, bald cap, mastix, latex, derma wax, rich moisturiser, spatula, cream make-up (all colours), eye shadow (turquoise, grey, brown), red eye pencil, white or very pale cake make-up or foundation, theatrical blood, vampire fangs, costume, blood capsules, special effects lenses.

If you want a bald vampire, use a bald cap (see the section on bald caps, on page 64). In this particular case, the model is already bald.

To get pointed ears, you can use a pair of latex ears. Here, the ear extensions are modelled directly onto the ears using derma wax (see fig. 1). Soften the wax and mix in a little rich moisturiser. Form the pointed extension of the ears using a spatula. Finish the derma wax work before applying make-up, as the derma-wax won't stick properly on top of make-up. Now colour the ears with skin-coloured, light brown and reddish cream make-up (see fig. 2).

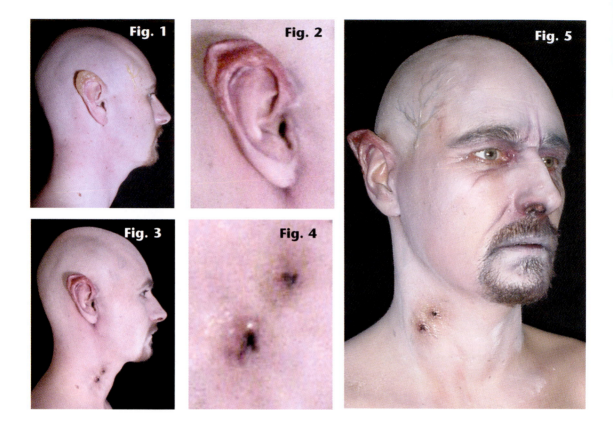

Fig. 1 Fig. 2 Fig. 3 Fig. 4 Fig. 5

If the vampire has been created by being bitten by Dracula or another vampire, the model must have two bite holes on the neck.

Make these in the same way as you would two flat bullet holes (see the section on bullet entrance holes, page 19) separated by the distance between two fangs (see figs 3 and 4): it's important to observe the correct distance here. Around the punctures, paint twisted veins using turquoise eye shadow and blend into the surrounding skin.

The facial make-up is done in the same way as for the well-dressed Dracula; make up eye surroundings, wrinkles and lips as described

above. Emphasise bags under the eyes more though, to give a more frightening appearance. Tint the nostrils with black cream make-up to make them more animal-like. With a thin brush, paint little veins moving upwards around the temples using turquoise (see fig. 5).

Dress the vampire in a costume such as an old suit covered in dust and cobwebs, or in gothic-style garments.

Let a little blood run from the corner of the mouth, to indicate that the vampire has just bitten someone (see fig. 6). For an event or a play, you can use little blood capsules:

conceal a capsule inside your mouth and break it with your teeth at an appropriate time. You can then let the blood run out of the corner of your mouth. Don't forget to wear fangs!

You can also wear scary special effects contact lenses, e.g. red bloodshot eyes, or completely white eyes with little black specks as pupils. It is also possible to get special lenses like the ones used in the film *Interview with the Vampire* (read more about contact lenses on page 75).

Children's painted Dracula

This Dracula is done as a face-paint mask. Paint the face and neck pale with white water-based make-up, and paint black around the eyes. Tone around the eyes using a sponge to make the eyes look deep-set. Paint the eyebrows black and bushy, colour the hair black and make a point going down the middle of the forehead. Paint two vertical lines between the eyebrows to give an angry expression. Paint the mouth blood-red with white fangs.

Examples of relevant film titles:

Nosferatu, Eine Symphonie des Grauens (1922) – English title: *Nosferatu*
Dracula (1931)
Hammer's *Dracula* (1958)
The Horror of Dracula / The Return of Dracula (1958)
Kiss of the Vampire (1962)
Dance of the Vampire (1967)
Nosferatu the Vampire (1979)
Salems Lot (1979)
The Hunger (1983)
Fright Night (1985)

Fig. 6

The Lost Boys (1987)
Waxwork (1988)
Fright Night Part II (1989)
Chronos (1992)
Innocent Blood (1992)
Bram Stoker's Dracula (1992)
Interview with the Vampire (1995)
From Dusk to Dawn (1996)
Julia (1998)
Blade (1999)
The Shadow of the Vampire (2001)

Zombie

The word 'zombie' means: a corpse reanimated by supernatural forces; a strange and apathetic person. The concept of zombies comes from Haiti's Voodoo religion, a mystic cult led by the Houngan and Hunzo priests and the priestess Mambo. The inaugural ceremony is long and arduous and includes ritual dances, where the dancers reach a state of ecstasy, and the sacrificing of goats and chickens.

According to the cult of Voodoo, a zombie is a cursed person, who has been poisoned by the secret poison of a Voodoo priest. The person is paralysed, slides into a trance-like state and is declared dead by the local doctor. The vital body functions are reduced to an activity level too weak to measure, but the senses of sight and vision are still acute. A ceremonial funeral convinces the family that the person really is dead, but about 24 hours after the burial – before the oxygen in the coffin runs out – the person is dug up. The person is given a kind of antidote, which to a certain extent reawakens the vital functions of the body, allowing it to work at a reduced pace, but the will is weakened. Legend has it that in earlier times, a person who had become a zombie was used for slave labour on the plantation-owner's fields.

This myth about officially dead people, seen wandering about restlessly at night, has been exploited by film-makers, who have transformed the zombie into foamy-mouthed, bloody and decaying monsters who eat human flesh. These zombies are usually subject to fixed rules: a zombie cannot be killed unless you knock or shoot its head off; zombies move sluggishly and do not react to pain; zombies eat the flesh, entrails and brains of humans; someone who is wounded by a zombie and survives will die slowly and then become a zombie. In films, zombies are created in bizarre Voodoo rituals

or with a mysterious poison, which awakens the dead.

You can make up a zombie in a number of ways. A typical interpretation has decaying skin, often with bloody wounds and gouged eyes, and is clad in cerements or ordinary clothes which are bloodstained, torn to shreds and covered in dust, earth and maggots. One arm may be hanging from a shred of bloody skin and the eyes have a cold and staring expression.

In the following descriptions, a procedure for using latex, cotton wool and derma wax and a method for using gelatine are outlined.

Materials:

Brushes, spatula, bowls, cream make-up (pale yellow, red, blue, black and yellow), latex, cotton wool, gelatine powder, boiling water, glycerine, hairdryer, theatrical blood, blood paste, dark red eye pencil, Vaseline.

The following materials are optional: bald cap and mastix, artificial eye, locks of hair, black and/or red tooth lacquer.

If you want wounds and gashes on the head itself, use a bald cap (see the section on bald caps, page 64. In this particular case, the model is already bald. Using cream make-up, colour the bald cap (or the crown itself) and face a corpse-like yellow. If the model has hair and you're not using a bald cap, only make up the face.

The gelatine method

Mix 6–7 tbsp of powdered gelatine with boiling water in a bowl. Stir until you get a porridge-like consistency, and cool until lukewarm. Put a towel around the model's shoulders, and place two cotton pads over one eye and eyebrow. Using a spoon, carefully apply some gelatine mixture to the cotton pads, the forehead and the top of the cheek. The gelatine must cover the pads completely. Carefully form a hollow for the artificial eye slightly below the real eye. Also apply gelatine to other areas of the face and the bald crown. You can form threads with the gelatine to simulate dissolved skin. Avoid getting gelatine too close to the hairline, eyebrows and facial hair. Mount an artificial eye in the hollow, and apply a little gelatine mixture around the eye to make it look like the eye has drifted down the cheek slightly. Dry the gelatine mask with cold air from a hairdryer; hot air will simply melt the gelatine again. When the gelatine is dry and doesn't rub off, you can start colouring it.

The latex, cotton wool and derma wax method

While the model keeps their eyes closed, place cotton wool in a circle around one eye. Smooth the edges nicely into the skin with a little liquid latex, using a spatula. Place small strips of cotton wool on the skin and shape them into cuts and gashes. Keep smoothing

the cotton wool using latex. Dry with a hairdryer at regular intervals (see fig. 1).

Soften small pieces of derma wax and roll them into little cylinders. Shape these into several scars and cuts around the zombie's face and head (see page 10 for more on making bloody wounds with derma wax). Mount an artificial eye over the model's real eye, or slightly further down. Lay a cylinder of derma wax around the eye as eyelids and smooth the edges. You can also make the lids out of cotton wool and liquid latex (see fig. 2). When all the latex is completely dry, you can start painting the mask.

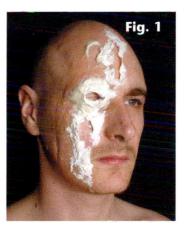

Fig. 1

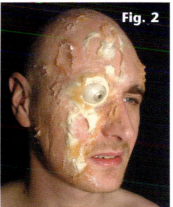

Fig. 2

Colouring

Paint the face in reddish, brownish, skin-coloured, bluish, black and yellow cream make-up colours. Paint flesh showing through the skin on the face, with red and bluish tones. Paint hollows and gashes black or reddish to give a deep and bloody look (see fig. 3). Colour the wet ridge of the real eye's lower eyelid dark red with an eye pencil to give a sickly appearance.

Affix thin locks of hair to the zombie's head with mastix. If the zombie is to have suppurating wounds, put a little glycerine or Vaseline mixed with a little yellow cream make-up in the wound as pus. Use theatrical blood and blood paste where the zombie has open cuts, and especially around the gouged eye (see fig. 4). You can also paint the teeth with black and red tooth lacquer.

Costume and staging

Use a white sheet with a hole cut in it for cerements and apply theatrical blood. If you want, you can also cut a hole in the stomach area and let artificial entrails, e.g. bowels, hang out of it. You can also make up hands and arms, as described above for the face, using cotton wool, gelatine, cream make-up and theatrical blood. Let the zombie hump along, while chewing on an artificial arm (see page 28 on artificial limbs and page 45 on artificial entrails).

Zombies don't talk but emit plaintive moans and groans. In the film series, *Return of the Living Dead*, the dead are just about able to say: 'Brains, brains' to express their appetite for human brains.

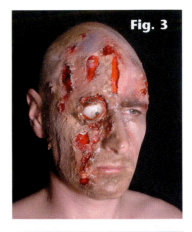

Fig. 3

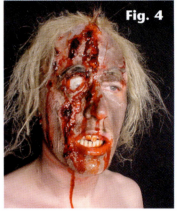

Fig. 4

If both the zombie's eyes are intact, a pair of special effects contact lenses may prove a good investment. These could be blind-white, entirely black or yellow-red flame-eyes.

To get an idea of how different kinds of zombies look, I recommend watching a couple of zombie-films:

Examples of relevant films:
Plague of the Zombies (1966)
Night of the Living Dead (1968 & 1990)
Dawn of the Dead (1979)
Zombie Flesh Eaters (1979)
Zombie Holocaust (1980)
The Gates of Hell (1980)
The Beyond (1981)
Thriller (1983) – Michael Jackson music video
Day of the Dead (1985)
Return of the Living Dead I, II, & III (1985, 1987, 1993)
The Rainbow & the Serpent (1989)
Braindead (1992)

The monster of the future may turn out to be an evil artificial human with built-in machine parts. This kind of monster has already been portrayed in films and literature.

A Cyborg is a 'cybernetic organism' or unity between a human and his technical extension; half man, half machine. The word was invented in 1960 by two scientists, Manfred E. Clynes and Nathan Kline. They introduced an osmotic pump into the metabolic system of a white rat, thereby creating the world's first cyborg. In 1998, professor Kevin Warwick claimed to be the world's first human cyborg. He had inserted a computer chip 21 mm long into his arm; with this, he was able to control various mechanisms in his home, as well as his computer.

In the world of film, a terminator is a humanoid robot or cyborg, created for the purpose of killing (terminating life). The first film containing a humanoid robot was Fritz Lang's *Metropolis*, made in 1922, in which a woman is transformed into a robot. Today, the best known cyborg must be the terminator played by Arnold Schwarzenegger in the films: *The Terminator*, T*erminator 2: Judgement Day*, and *Terminator 3: Rise of the Machines*.

Both cyborgs and terminators can be created in a variety of ways. This section deals with the two most common methods.

Terminator

Materials:
Derma wax, spatula, rich moisturiser, water-based or cream make-up (silver or metallic, white, black, red), brushes, theatrical blood, a red special effects contact lens (optional).

Roll several derma-wax cylinders and apply these to the face, splitting it into two halves separated by a vertical derma-wax wound in the middle. Smooth the wax edge on the unscathed half of the face using a spatula, and fray the edge on the other side – the robot side (see fig. 1). Paint the inside of the frayed wax edge dark red, to simulate blood under the torn-off skin (see fig. 2): the idea is to make it look like the skin has been pulled away from part of the face, revealing a metal robot skull. Colour the robot-half using silver or metallic make-up, and add shadowing and highlighting using black and white, to emphasise metal edges and robot structure (see fig. 3).

Paint little rivets and screws, by simply painting a black speck with a smaller white speck on, representing reflected light. Take your time and paint the rivets evenly and in regular lines or patterns, to get the best possible result (see fig. 4). Dab a little theatrical blood onto the frayed edge of the skin which divides the face, and allow it to

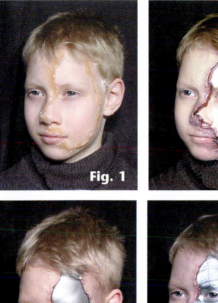
Fig. 1
Fig. 2

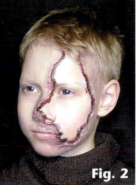

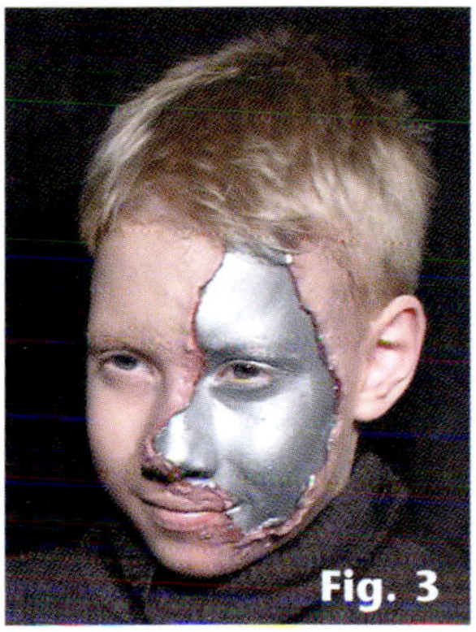

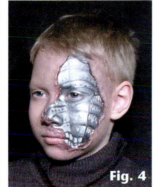
Fig. 3
Fig. 4

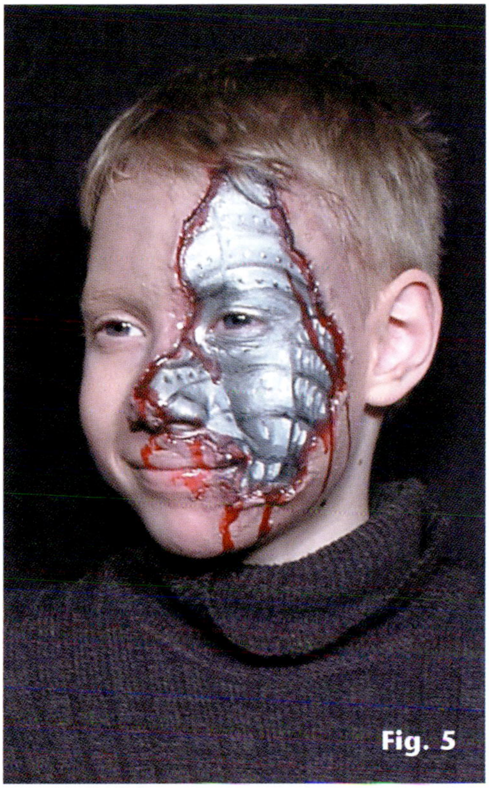

Fig. 5

run down the cheek a little for dramatic effect (see fig. 5). A special effects contact lens, either red or grey with printed circuits, would suit the robot part of the face perfectly and be a nice finishing touch. Otherwise, paint the eyelids red on the robot part of the face.

You can also do this terminator make-up as pure face paint, especially if it is for children. Instead of the derma-wax edge, paint a black frayed edge with water-based make-up. Paint the metal side, along with structure and rivets, in the same way as described above. Use red water-based make-up for blood.

Cyborg

There are many different kinds of cyborgs. Technically, a cyborg is a human with technology implanted under the skin. Most film-cyborgs have a kind of electronic eye instead of one of their eyes; this norm will be followed in the descriptions of cyborg make-up given on the following pages.

Materials:

Cotton pads, derma wax, spatula, cotton wool, latex, a small bowl, an objective lens from an old camera or binoculars, electrical wires, electronic components, hairdryer, cream make-up (red, skin-coloured, brownish silver and metallic), foundation, theatrical blood.

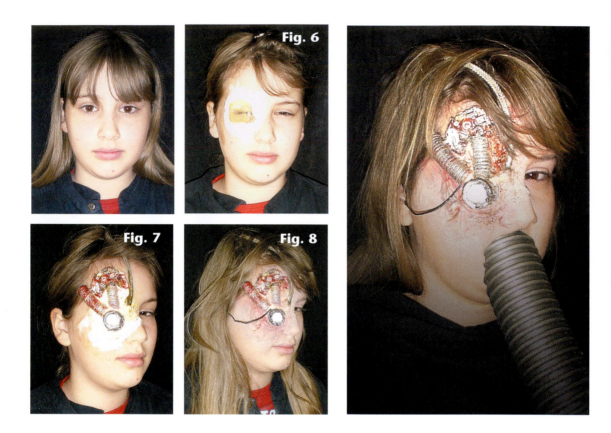

Fig. 6

Fig. 7

Fig. 8

Roll two derma-wax cylinders, and place one of them directly under one eyebrow, and the other directly under the same eye. Press the wax firmly into place. Place a cotton pad over the wax cylinders, so that it covers the eye and eyebrow, and press it firmly into place. Carefully apply little pieces of cotton wool dipped in liquid latex to the area on and around the cotton pads, letting them come down onto the cheek slightly. Avoid getting liquid latex in the eyes and be careful not to drip latex on your clothes. Smooth the surface of the latex and cotton wool with a spatula (see fig. 6). Form a kind of bowl-shaped socket in the cotton wool and mount the objective lens to simulate an electronic eye. Smooth the adjoining edges using latex

and cotton wool, and mount a few electrical wires or electronic components so they stick out of the cotton wool or the latex skin. If you have difficulty concealing the cotton wool edges, smooth them with a little derma wax. Dry the latex with a hairdryer (see fig. 7). When the latex is dry, colour the deformed skin around the object lens with skin-coloured, brownish and reddish cream make-up or foundation. Use theatrical blood as well. You can also fix the ends of the wires to other areas of skin using a little derma wax (see fig. 8). If you like, add a little blood here and there. Find a suitable hairstyle and costume.

Monsters come from dark corners, caves, outer space, old houses and, last but not least, from our imagination. Monsters can also come from underwater – a lagoon, for instance.

1954 saw the introduction of a new monster, which caught and devoured beautiful young women to the horror of film audiences. In the film *The Creature from the Black Lagoon* the actor Ben Chupman was dressed up as the scaly prehistoric monster, who abducts actress Julie Adams. The creature underwent many changes and modifications in Universal Studio's make-up department before the final appearance for the creature was fully developed. The costume was a body stocking with thick pads of painted foam-rubber glued to it, and it took 2–3 people more than 2 hours to put the costume on the actor. The monster of the 50s was born, and remains a favourite to this day.

Several versions of reptile men have since appeared on the silver screen: here is my version.

Snout-piece

Reptiles don't have round heads with a nose like humans do, but a rather more flat and oblong head, which is quite far from human in shape. Therefore, I have opted for a hybrid form; a reptile human. For this, we need a mask-piece, which will function as the creature's snout. There are many ways of making one of these: the method described here is both easy and cheap. All you need is a little cotton wool and liquid latex, the rest is sheer paintwork.

Materials:
Glass bust, plasticine, spatula, cotton wool, latex, a little bubble plastic (the kind you use to wrap fragile things in), hairdryer, scissors, cream make-up (all colours), mastix or prostick, water-based make-up (all colours).

The following materials are optional: bald cap, brushes, card templates for scales, airbrush or eye shadow, make-up brushes.

Shape the snout-piece on a glass bust, using cotton wool. Place the cotton wool over the top of the nose and mouth of the bust, gradually building it up into a reptile snout. Using a spatula, smooth the cotton wool at regular intervals with liquid latex (see fig. 1) – look in a book on reptiles for inspiration. Cut the bubble plastic into little patches and place them at strategic points on the snout. The result will be that the snout has a bubble plastic surface (see fig. 2).

Fig. 1

Fig. 2

Give the whole thing a couple of layers of liquid latex and dry with a hairdryer. You should end up with a yellowish surface that has a reptilian look (see fig. 3).

Powder well after the final layer of latex, and carefully remove the latex part from the glass bust (see fig. 4). Trim the edges of the snout to get a nice even edge (see fig. 5): now the snout-piece is ready for colouring with cream make-up in green or brownish tones (see figs 6 and 7). You can also leave the colouring of the nose until it is mounted on the model. When you have finished colouring the nose, all you have to do is powder it, and then it's ready for use.

Affix the nose-piece to the model with mastix or prostick (see figs 9 and 10). If the border between the nose-piece and the skin is too conspicuous, conceal it with small pieces of toilet paper dipped in latex, which are then left to dry.

Now put a bald cap on the actor. Put some cotton wool underneath the bald cap to make the forehead higher – this will make the shape of the head look less human (see fig. 11).

Fig. 5

Fig. 6

Fig. 7

Fig. 8

Fig. 9

Fig. 10

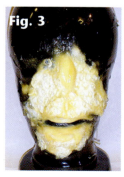
Fig. 3

Fig. 4

Fig. 11

Fig. 12

The rest of the work is pure face-painting, which you can do with water-based make-up. Paint the face in shades of green, alternating between light and dark greens to get a more varied and realistic colour. Reptile eyes are more at the side of the head than human eyes, so you can paint large round eyes on the model's temples. Most reptiles have snake-like eyes, i.e. yellow or green with an oblong, perpendicular pupil. Because of the painted eyes, the actor must keep their eyes closed so that the creature doesn't have four eyes (see fig. 12).

Another possibility for eyes is to make a pair of reptile eyes out of polystyrene balls (see page 32 for instructions on making artificial eyes). (When designing these, it's a good idea to do a bit of research in relevant books.) You can make a small hole in the middle of the polystyrene eyes for the model to see through: the hole must be in the middle of the pupil, and doesn't have to be very big to allow the actor clear vision.

You must also paint the ears. Paint scales using a thin brush and outline them in black. The scales can either be hexagonal, forming a beehive-like pattern, or they can be semi-circular, each row slightly overlapping the next. You may want to make a cardboard template; then you can use an airbrush, or apply eye shadow through the template with a make-up brush. You might want to make templates of different sizes, to add variation to the scales (see figs 13 and 14). Paint a little light reflection on each scale with white water-based make-up or an airbrush; this will make the whole surface come alive.

When reptiles change their skin, the old skin trails after the animal until it has loosened itself completely, revealing the new skin. To simulate this, pour a little latex onto a smooth surface. Spread the latex so you get a thin layer the size of the skin you want. Allow to dry at room temperature, or use a hairdryer. Thoroughly powder the latex and loosen it, while powdering underneath. It doesn't matter if the latex-skin becomes a little frayed and broken. Crumple the latex slightly and affix it with mastix to the area of loosening skin. Let the edges of the skin remain slightly loose and make the colour of the new skin a slightly darker shade. This will create the impression of new and fresh skin underneath the loosened skin.

A finished mask made out of cotton wool and latex.

Fig. 13 Fig. 14

People have always been fascinated by stories about resurrecting the dead. The most famous of these is the story of Frankenstein's monster.

The novel *Frankenstein* was written by Mary Shelley in 1816–1817, when she was just 19 years old. This famous book has inspired theatre plays, movies, TV films, comic books, and further novels. The story is about a scientist who creates a living being from parts of dead bodies. Dr Frankenstein's hunchbacked assistant Fritz goes out at night and steals the body parts from churchyards and mortuaries. By mistake, Fritz steals the brain of an insane criminal, which ends up being used for Frankenstein's creature. Using lightning for electricity, Dr Frankenstein succeeds in giving his creature life – but to his great dismay, the monster has a completely different personality from what he had expected.

There are many ways of doing Frankenstein's monster make-up. The method described here is slightly unusual, as silicone is used for making a mould. However, an alternative and simpler method using a bald cap is also described.

Model Frankenstein's characteristic high forehead with plasticine on a glass bust. Start by modelling a rough version (see fig. 1) and then work in more detail. Use a spatula to scrape details in the plasticine, such as wrinkles and lines in the skin. Dab the plasticine with a rough sponge to get a skin-like surface structure (see fig. 2). You can also model hair on top of the crown using thin plasticine cylinders (see fig. 3). When you are satisfied with your modelling, the mould is ready for use.

Fig. 1

Fig. 2

Fig. 3

Materials:

A bald cap, a glass or plastic bust, cotton wool, latex, silicone mass (Castogel), glass bowl, spatula, black crepe hair or similar, plasticine, mastix or prostick, derma wax, pale yellow foundation, face powder or talc, cream make-up (all colours), theatrical blood, eye shadow (grey, red and brown), crepe hair, a costume (optional).

Fig. 4

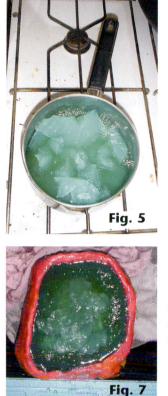

Fig. 5

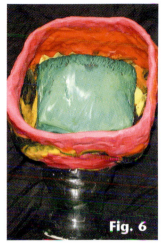

Fig. 6

Fig. 7

You can cool it near an open window or in the fridge.

In the meantime, shape a wall around the modelled monster forehead. You can make the wall out of ordinary plasticine, which you can buy in toy shops (see fig. 6). Make sure that the wall is completely watertight.

Now, carefully pour the lukewarm Castogel into the monster forehead mould (see fig. 7). Leave the whole thing to harden for a couple of hours.

Place the mould between some heavy objects to prevent it from toppling over.

Normally you use casting plaster to make moulds, but to demonstrate another kind of casting material we will use a silicone mass called Castogel (see fig. 4). Castogel has the advantage that it can be melted in an ordinary saucepan and hardens again at room temperature. Break off some pieces of the Castogel mass and put them in a saucepan. Stir with an old wooden spoon until the mass has melted (see fig. 5). For health reasons, use a saucepan which is no longer used for cooking. Melt at low temperature, otherwise the Castogel will give off smoke and an unpleasant smell. When the Castogel has melted completely, cool to a temperature of approximately 40°C/100°F.

When the Castogel-silicone has hardened completely, carefully remove the plasticine and the silicone mould from the glass bust (see fig. 8). The silicone may break.

Fig. 8

Castogel is good for making detailed moulds, but must be handled with care or it may break.

Now apply liquid latex to the silicone negative-mould with a brush, and dry at intervals with a hairdryer. Apply 4–5 layers of latex in total (see fig. 9).

When the final layer is dry, carefully lift the latex forehead off the silicone mould (see fig. 10). Test it on the model or the glass bust to see if it fits. To strengthen the higher part of the forehead, put a little cotton wool on the inside and use some liquid latex to secure the cotton wool (see fig. 11). When the latex and cotton wool on the inside is dry, the forehead is ready for colouring. Mount the forehead on the glass bust (see fig. 12) and colour it using cream or rubber make-up in various skin-colours (see fig. 13).

An easier method

Mount a ready-made bald cap on a bust or something similar. Dip little pieces of cotton wool in a bowl of latex and build up an extension of the forehead all the way round, so that the top part of the head becomes higher. Smooth the cotton wool and latex with a spatula, so the transition to the bald cap doesn't show. When you are satisfied with the shape and height of the cotton wool–latex extension, dry the whole thing with a hairdryer. The cotton wool–latex mass is dry when it turns a yellowish colour. Then, affix locks of black crepe hair or a very short black wig with bristly hairs to the cotton wool–latex crown and leave to dry once more. In the same way, model the arch of the

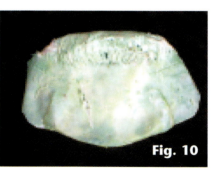

Fig. 9

Fig. 10

If necessary, remove any remaining bits of plasticine and silicone from the latex part before continuing the modelling work.

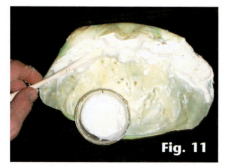

Fig. 11

Fig. 12

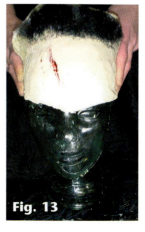

Fig. 13

forehead on the bust using cotton wool and latex. If you like, you can also stitch all the way across the forehead with black sewing thread, so it looks like it has been sewn on. When all the cotton wool–latex parts are completely dry, powder them with talc or face powder and remove them from the bust.

Putting it on the forehead-piece

Mount the forehead-piece or the bald cap on the model's head, and glue the edges all the way round with mastix, latex or prostick (see fig. 14). Now make up the model's face, neck and ears using a pale yellow foundation or cream make-up. Make artificial eyebrows out of crepe hair and glue them on using mastix (see fig. 15). Powder the made-up area. Now, lay shadowing on the face. To make the eyes look deeper-set, shadow with a greyish-brown and blend into the natural edge of the eye hollows. Using greyish-brown eye shadow, make up wrinkles on the forehead, wrinkles around the eyes, lines around the mouth and bags under the eyes. Tint the area around the stitches, and the edge of the bald cap and forehead-piece, with a little reddish eye shadow or cream make-up. Colour the lips a brownish red (see fig. 16).

Affix two bolts to the sides of the neck with the help of a little derma wax. Press a softened piece of derma wax onto the side of the neck and smooth the edges with a spatula. Press an appropriately sized bolt into the wax: if the bolts are too heavy they won't stay in place and will eventually fall off.

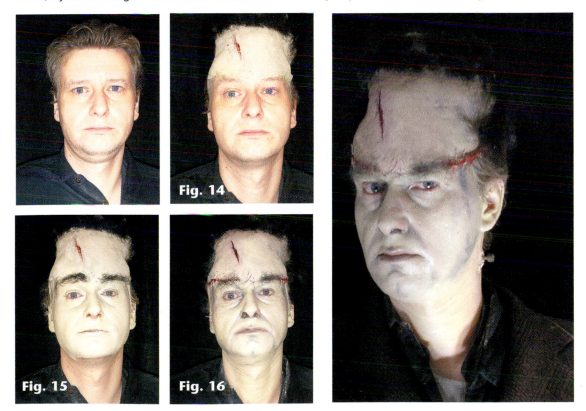

Fig. 14

Fig. 15

Fig. 16

Frankenstein's costume is a thick dark suit made of flax or another coarse material. The shoes are a dark colour and enormously large.

The most well-known appearance of Frankenstein's monster must be the one played by Boris Karloff, who played the monster in several horror films in the 1930s. In the 1994 film *Mary Shelley's Frankenstein*, Robert De Niro played a somewhat different version of the famous monster.

In some interpretations, Dr Frankenstein's monster is portrayed as having green skin – especially in comic books and cartoons. Described below is an easy-to-do monster make-up for children:

Frankenstein's monster as face-paint

Materials:
Brushes, water-based make-up (various greens, black), theatrical blood, black eye pencil, a tatty suit (optional).

Paint the model's face, ears and neck verdigris green with water-based make-up. Tint the eye surroundings a darker colour using black water-based make-up, to make them look more hollow. Colour a dark shadow at the bottom of the forehead to create the impression of a protruding forehead. Paint bags under the eyes, and lines around the eyes and on the forehead. Tint shadows around the corners of the mouth and below the wing of the nose. Paint thick, bushy eyebrows with black water-based make-up. Paint a vertical gash on the right side of the monster's forehead, and let a

little theatrical blood or dark red water-based make-up run from the wound. At the top of the forehead directly below the hairline, draw stitches with a black eye pencil, so it looks as though the head has been sewn together.

Frankenstein's monster has black hair, so colour the hair black with water-based make-up, or use a black, shorthaired wig. For the costume, use a thick dark suit made of flax or a similar coarse material. The shoes should be dark in colour and enormously large.

Examples of relevant films:
Frankenstein (1931)
Bride of Frankenstein (1935)
Son of Frankenstein (1939)
House of Frankenstein (1944)
Frankenstein: The True Story (1973)
Young Frankenstein (1974)
Bride of Frankenstein (1985)
Frankenstein Unbound (1990)
Frankenstein (1992)
Mary Shelley's Frankenstein (1994)

Without evil in some form or other, most films and plays would probably be terribly boring. Not that you can't have a good story solely about good things, but a touch of evil always adds to the drama.

The horned god has had many different representations through the ages. The common denominator for most versions is that he is evil, with horns and a tail. The typical depiction of the devil as a goat-like figure is actually an invention of the church: before the spread of Christianity, there were various 'nature' religions. One of them involved the worship of a horned god and the maternal goddess Gaia. Gaia was a name for mother earth, and the god of fertility was a horned figure whom people worshipped to secure the harvest and have many children. They chose to give the horned god the form of a goat, and priests wore a goat-like costume for religious festivals. While a new religion is taking over, the waning religion is usually classified as evil – thus, the horned god of fertility was transformed into the devil with the legs of a goat, a tail and horns. Since then, fairytales, myths, stories and superstition in folklore have reinforced this perception and continue to do so today. The devil remains a common figure in fairytales, theatre, literature, films, TV and comic books.

Put a ready-made bald cap on the model's head and glue it in place. Make sure that the bald cap is glued all the way round (see page 64 on bald caps – and fig. 1).

Affix a pair of pointed ears, ready-made or home-made (see page 42 on making artificial ears). In this case, you build up the ears using toilet paper soaked in a bit of latex. Shape the latex-soaked paper mass into the desired ear-shape and put them over the model's real ears. The latex itself is enough to hold them in place when dried with a hairdryer (see fig. 2). Make a pointed nose in the same way.

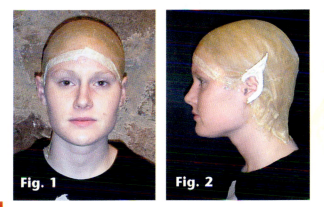

Fig. 1   **Fig. 2**

Materials:

Bald cap, mastix or prostick, latex, latex horns, toilet paper, hairdryer, water-based make-up (red, black), black crepe hair or an artificial moustache and pointed chin-beard. The following are optional: latex ears and nose, dark grey eye shadow, brushes, red eye pencil.

Affix a pair of latex horns, ready-made or homemade, to the temples (see page 38 on making horns and noses. Use mastix, prostick or latex to glue the horns on. If the edges of the horns are too conspicuous, cover them with small pieces of toilet paper dipped in latex (see fig. 3).

Paint the model's face, ears, neck and the bald cap dark red with water-based make-up (see figs 3 and 4). Shadow around the eyes with grey-black water-based make-up or eye shadow, making the eyes look deep-set. Paint the eyebrows using black water-based make-up or dark grey eye shadow. Ask the model to frown so that the natural lines between the eyebrows become apparent. Emphasise these lines, and the lines on the forehead and the fine wrinkles on the bridge of the nose, with grey eye shadow. Tone the wrinkles into the surrounding skin, to make them look more realistic – i.e. tone horizontal lines so they fade out towards the top, and let the bottom edge of the line remain sharp. Furthermore, paint bags under the eyes, lines running from the wing of the nose down past the mouth and hollow cheeks. Paint the wet rim of the lower eyelid with a dark-red eye pencil.

Affix an artificial beard. The sides of the moustache should continue down the sides of the mouth to join the pointed chin-beard or goatee (see page 60 on making artificial beards). If the model already has a beard, you might be able to simply trim this to the right shape. You can glue on the artificial beard using mastix, prostick or latex. Apply the glue below the nose while the model holds their breath; mount the moustache and hold it in place until the glue is dry. Mount the chin-beard in the same way (see fig. 5).

A pair of yellow cat's eyes contact lenses will make the devil even more convincing (read more about contact lenses on page 75).

The devil's costume can be either furry, leather or suede trousers and a bare torso (in which case you'll also have to paint the torso and arms), or black clothes and a black cloak.

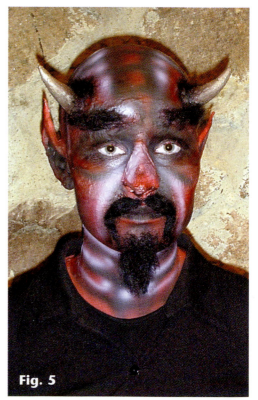
Fig. 5

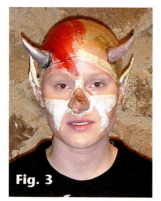
Fig. 3

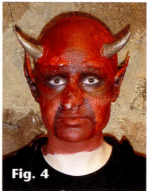
Fig. 4

Appropriate props are a prong and/or a skull, which the devil holds in his or her hand.

Relevant film titles:
Rosemary's Baby (1968)
The Exorcist (1973)
Amityville I - IV (1976, 1982, 1983, 1992)
The Omen (1976)
Krull (1983)
Legend (1985)
Prince of Darkness (1987)
Highway to Hell (1991)

You can paint a skull directly on the face, or use a mask. When making up a person to look like a skull, the result will be slightly larger than actual size, as what is supposed to be inside the head is actually on the outside of the head.

Materials:
Bald cap, mastix or prostick, latex, water-based make-up (white, black and yellow), dark grey eye shadow, brushes.

You can paint a skull directly on the face, or use a mask. When making up a person to look like a skull, the result will be slightly larger than actual size, as what is supposed to be inside the head is actually on the outside of the head.

Start by studying the anatomy of a skull in a medical book or an encyclopaedia of anatomy.

Put the bald cap on the model, making sure that it is glued all the way round the edges (see page 64 on bald caps – and fig. 1). Paint the model black around the eyes with water-based make-up. Follow the natural contours of the eye-hollows. Paint the outlines of the mouth and the mouth area in black, and the nasal cavity above the wings of the nose as an inverted 'V', so that you get a hollow with a strip of bone down the middle where the nose is. Paint the rest of the face and the bald cap white (see fig. 2). Paint in details like teeth and cheekbones. If you like, paint the teeth an uneven yellow to give the impression of the teeth being old. Outline the teeth using a thin brush to show where they protrude from the skull. Then tint shadows from the teeth up to the cheekbone.

Now lay the various shadows, marking the shape and contours of the skull, using dark-grey eye shadow: concave temples, a hollow between the eyes, shading on the cheekbones, jawbones and on the crown. Draw fissures on the crown and temples of the skull with an eye pencil and also irregularities in the surface structure of the skull in general (see figs 3 and 4).

You can also paint the neck black with the discs of the spine in the middle.

Fig. 1

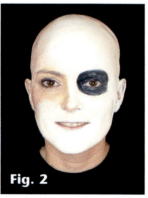

Fig. 2

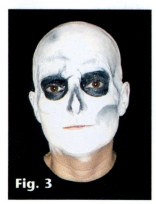

Fig. 3

Fig. 4

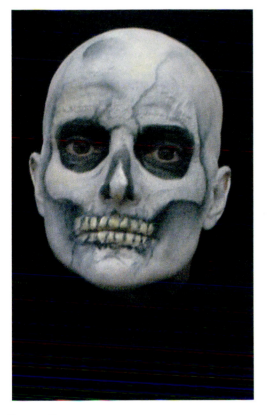

Paint black around the eyes and an inverted 'V' on the nose. Colour the rest of the face white with water-based make-up. Paint the skull's teeth onto the lips using liquid eyeliner and black water-based make-up. Paint the teeth all the way out to the dimples on the cheeks; they can be tinted a yellowish colour. Paint a dark shadow above the teeth, continuing this shadow up to below the cheekbones where it narrows into a thin line, which continues sideways up to the temples. Paint fissures and cracks around the eyes and add a little blood running from one eye or the mouth, for additional dramatic effect.

Suggestion:
If you want more three-dimensional teeth, you can make artificial teeth out of cernit and bake them in the oven at 130°C/250°F/gas mark 1. Glue the teeth onto the lips using mastix or prostick. If you like, paint between the teeth with black water-based make-up.

Skull as an easy-to-do face-paint for children

Film-makers and writers of horror stories are constantly searching for new monsters to frighten the living daylights out of us. Pinhead is one of these latter-day monsters, created by Clive Barker.

Hellraiser is a film about the invocation of demons, and Pinhead, as he is called (played by Doug Bradley), is the leader of these demons. The demons are called Cenobites and they relish shredding their victims with meat hooks, which handily enough come down from the ceiling in chains. He who seeks the ultimate thrill can turn a kind of magic dice and open the gates to Pinhead's terrifying world.

Pinhead's stooges (one more scary than the other) aid him in creating terror and havoc. Pinhead himself, who has had nails inserted in his head and face, making him look like an animated pin-cushion, is a kind of antichrist figure. At the time of writing, *Hellraiser* – based on a novel by Clive Barker and first adapted to film in 1992 – has had four sequels, the last of which takes place in outer space.

Pinhead is a little difficult to do. In this chapter, two methods of making the nail-studded head are described.

Method 1

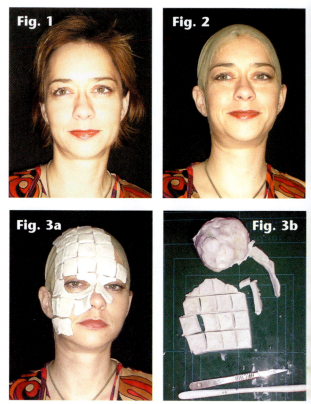

Fig. 1
Fig. 2
Fig. 3a
Fig. 3b

First, put an ordinary bald cap on the model and glue all the way round using mastix or prostick (see fig. 2).

Cut a lot of little flat squares out of white plasticine, and glue these onto the face and head, one next to the other, so they form a matrix. Trim the squares to fit around the nose and eyes (see figs 3a, 3b and 4). Press the squares lightly at intervals to make sure they don't fall off while the glue is still wet.

When all the squares are mounted and the glue is dry, paint the whole face a pale yellow colour with cream make-up. Paint the neck

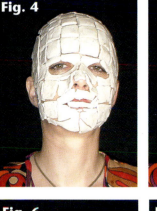

Fig. 4

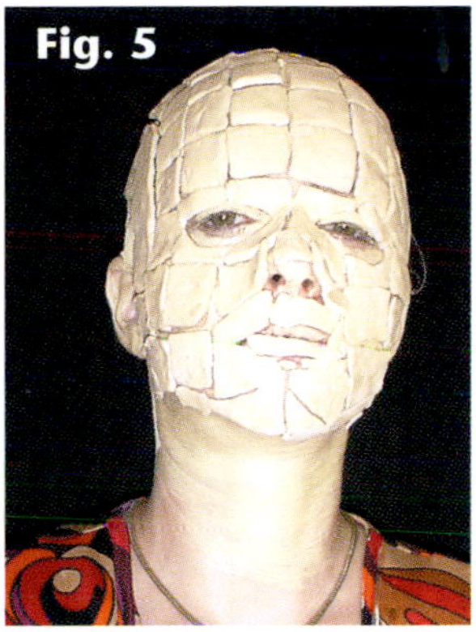

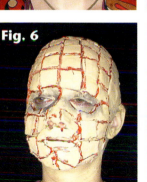

Fig. 6

Fig. 5

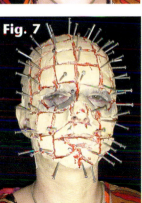

Fig. 7

and ears too (see fig. 5), then powder the whole face. Paint the gaps in between the squares a subdued grey shadow or blood-red as shown in figure 6.

Now you have to make a lot of specially prepared nails. Choose reasonably long nails but they mustn't be too heavy. Nip off all the points of the nails so that they are no longer sharp: you can do this with a pair of wire cutters. These nails will be mounted on the head and face, so it looks like they have been

hammered into the skull. Press the nails into the plasticine where the lines of the grid formed by the squares cross. Make sure they are pushed well into the plasticine but be careful not to hurt the model.

Once the mask is finished, it's important that you wear the right facial expression.

Method 2

> *Materials:*
> Bald cap, mastix, spatula, brushes, white plasticine, scalpel, chopping board, cream make-up (pale yellow, red, grey), face powder, plenty of nails and a pair of wire cutters.

Make a bald cap in the usual way (see page 64 on making bald caps), or use a ready-made bald cap. Paint it a pale yellow colour using cream make-up and/or foundation, giving it a corpse-like hue. Then powder it to prevent the colour from rubbing off. Turn the bald cap inside out and mount it on a glass bust. Draw a grid pattern with a dark-brown eye pencil. Remove the bald cap from the glass bust, and press the nails into the points where the lines cross, so that the points are inward and the heads stick out on the outside. Apply little pieces of cotton wool dipped in latex to the inside of the bald cap where the nails pierce the cap, to hold the nails in place. Dry the latex with a hairdryer. Then turn the bald cap right side out, and your Pinhead bald cap is ready for use.

Soften small pieces of derma wax and put them on the face in the same pattern as the bald-cap grid – also cover the nose, cheeks and chin (see fig. 4). Smooth each piece of derma wax, thereby concealing the transition from wax to skin and leaving only inconspicuous mounds on the skin. Colour Pinhead's face a pale yellow with cream make-up or foundation applied with a sponge – make sure the transition from bald cap to skin is well hidden by the make-up colour. Make up the eye hollows with grey eye shadow to make the eyes look deeper-set. Emphasise bags under the eyes. Now push a nail, point first, into each derma-wax mound.

Give the hands a pale colour using foundation or light yellow cream make-up as for the face. Pinhead wears a black leather suit with a high collar and holes cut in the chest area. To perfect the disguise use a pair of completely black special effects contact lenses.

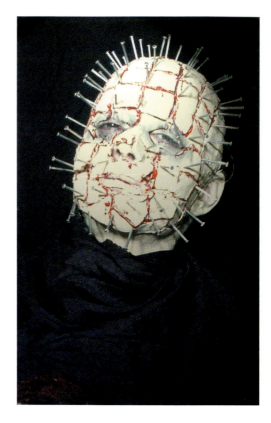

The series of films about Freddy Kruger, played by Robert Englund, are called *A Nightmare on Elm Street*. Freddie Kruger is a kind of nightmare murderer, who appears in his victims' dreams, and if they don't wake up in time, they are brutally murdered.

Freddie Kruger was the son of Amanda Kruger, who was held captive in a prison tower with hundreds of insane criminals. While there, Amanda was raped and Freddie conceived.

While Freddie was growing up, he attacked and murdered children in the Elm Street neighbourhood. The parents of these children caught Freddie and, taking the law into their own hands, set fire to him so he burned to death. Since then, Freddie's spirit has haunted Elm Street, and the descendants of the people who burned him are haunted in their dreams.

The film series *A Nightmare on Elm Street* consists of seven films altogether, and the last of these, *Wes Graven's Nightmare,* is about the film director's nightmares about the films that he himself has made. All these films are full of imaginative special effects. Especially notable are the scenes where Freddie assumes the form of various crazy things in people's dreams, such as a TV set, a giant Freddie-snake, a telephone receiver and – with his glove, on which sharp blades are mounted on each finger – he spreads fear and terror among his victims and the audience alike.

Materials:

Bald cap, brushes, spatula, bowls, glycerine, powdered gelatine or latex, cotton wool, hairdryer, cream make-up (black, brown, yellow, red), face powder or talc, theatrical blood, yellow tooth lacquer, kitchen roll or similar.

Freddie has burns on his entire face and head, and therefore you must use a bald cap (see page 64 on making and mounting bald caps). Put on the bald cap and glue the edges with mastix, latex or prostick (see fig. 1).

The next procedure can be done in two ways: using gelatine, or using cotton wool and latex.

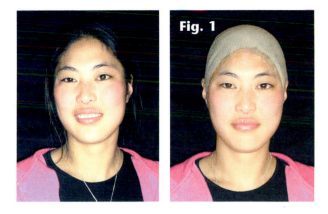

Fig. 1

If you use gelatine, mix powdered gelatine and boiling water in a bowl in a ratio of twice as much water as powder, so you get a thick, porridge-like substance. The gelatine is ready to use for modelling when it has cooled to room temperature. If you use cotton wool and latex, pour latex in a large bowl and add little pieces of cotton wool so that you get a thicker consistency. The latex–cotton wool mixture is ready for use right away.

Form burns and skin deformities as long, deep disfigurations (see fig. 2): be careful not to get latex or gelatine in the eyebrows, eyes or facial hair. During the modelling, you can smooth the burns with a spatula, so the disfigurements look softer and more realistic (see fig. 3). Don't use expensive, quality brushes when working with latex and gelatine. Treat the whole face, but avoid getting too close to the eyes and nostrils. When you have finished modelling, dry with cold air from a hairdryer.

Now paint the face using black, brown, yellow and red cream make-up. Paint hollows black and brown, and raised areas reddish and yellowish. Paint black around the eyes and paint the rest of the face a brownish red colour as if after burning (see figs 4 and 5). If you like, add a little theatrical blood to the paint and mix it in to give the face a horrific appearance (see figs 6a, 6b and 6c). Then powder with ordinary face powder or talc.

Fig. 2

Fig. 3

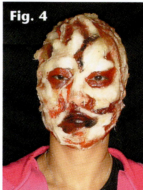
Fig. 4

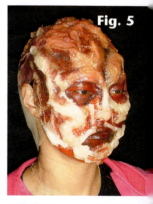
Fig. 5

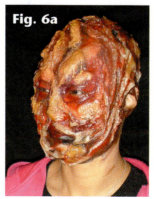
Fig. 6a

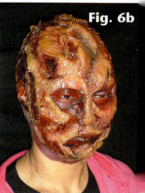
Fig. 6b

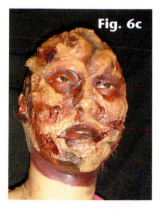

Fig. 6c

Dry the surface of the teeth with kitchen roll – they must be completely dry. The model must keep their mouth open until the work is done. Pour a little tooth lacquer onto the palm of your hand or a spatula. Apply the yellow lacquer directly onto the teeth with a thin brush, until you get an even colour. For hygienic reasons you shouldn't use the brush on the inside of the lid of the bottle. Let the tooth lacquer dry completely before the model closes their mouth.

Tooth lacquer can usually be removed simply by brushing the teeth. Note, however, that tooth varnish is a little difficult to wash off plastic teeth.

Freddie's costume is a thick red-and-black stripy sweater, and he usually wears a felt hat. On his right hand he wears a glove with a long metal blade on each finger.

Darth Maul

The famous space-epic *Star Wars* has introduced us to many fantastic monsters. One of the popular evil ones is Darth Maul.

Materials:

For this character you need a bald cap and six separate rubber horns (see page 64 on making bald caps, and page 38 on rubber horns). You can also use special effects contact lenses. You will also need: a spatula, mastix or prostick, brushes, cream make-up (yellow, brown), face powder or talc, water-based make-up (black, red, yellow).

The following are optional: black eye pencil, special effects contact lenses: yellow or volcano eyes, which are yellow in the middle and turn red toward the edges in a flame-like pattern.

In *Star Wars – Episode 1* we meet the Sith warrior Darth Maul, who is an apprentice of the Sith prince Darth Sidious. Darth Maul is a master of the two-bladed light sabre, and can fight two opponents simultaneously. The Sith order is a master-apprentice system which was established when a defected Jedi-knight wanted to gain control of the galaxy by using the Force, but was seduced by the 'dark side'. Darth Maul is bald and has horns, yellow eyes and black tattoos all over his face.

First colour the horns with yellow and brownish cream make-up, so they have a colour similar to ram's horns. Then powder the horns so the colour doesn't rub off.

Now trim the bald cap to shape and cut a piece away around the ears.

Paint the bald cap red: this can be done either before or after mounting the bald cap. Use a slightly darker than pillar-box red. Mount the bald cap and glue all the way around the edges, making sure that it is securely in place all over. Glue the horns on with mastix: one horn is at the front in the middle, like on a unicorn, and the others are on the sides (see fig. 1).

Paint the face red with water-based make-up. Don't paint the areas that are to be painted black – i.e. round the eyes, on the middle of the nose and around the corners of the mouth and on the cheeks. Make sure you get an even colour (see fig. 2). Now paint the black markings as shown in figures 3, 4 and 5. You may want to draw the outlines of the markings with a black eye pencil first to make sure you get a regular and symmetrical pattern.

Paint teeth on the lower lip with yellow water-based make-up, or paint directly onto the teeth with black and yellow tooth lacquer. To do this, dry the teeth with kitchen roll, put a little tooth lacquer on a spatula or the palm of your hand, and paint directly onto the teeth with a thin brush. For hygienic reasons, I advise against using the brush in the lid of the bottle. The model must keep their mouth open until the tooth lacquer is completely dry. Remove tooth varnish by brushing the teeth. Note, however, that it is

Fig. 1

Fig. 2

Fig. 3

Fig. 4

difficult to remove tooth lacquer from plastic teeth. As a final touch, use special effects lenses: yellow (not cat's eyes), or volcano-lenses, which are yellow in the middle and turn red towards the edges in a flame-like pattern.

Darth Maul wears a loose-fitting black felt costume, with a broad black scarf around the waist. He also wears long black leather gloves and black boots. For a light-sabre prop, buy a plastic light sabre in a toyshop. To create the double-bladed light sabre, you have to put two light sabres together by the handle and use black gaff tape to stick the two handles together.

Full moon is the time when werewolves go out hunting. A werewolf is a creature that is half man, half wolf.

In some tales, the werewolf only appears at full moon. In others, the werewolf can alternate between human and werewolf form at will. Someone who is attacked and wounded by a werewolf and survives, will themselves become a werewolf. Werewolves have supernatural strength and can be recognised in their human form because of the eyebrows being joined together. Most tales involve only a single werewolf spreading havoc and terror, but in the film *The Company of Wolves*, which is an interpretation of *Little Red Riding Hood*, many werewolves and ordinary wolves appear together. In most stories a werewolf can only be killed by silver bullets, but in others the werewolf is an ordinary mortal.

Making a latex snout

Materials:

Glass bust, plasticine, spatula, ordinary clay, casting plaster, bowl for mixing, latex, hairdryer, face powder or talc, cream make-up (black, brown, red, yellow, white), crepe hair in black and brown shades, whiskers or hairs from a brush.

Shape a snout on a glass bust using plasticine. Press an appropriately sized piece of plasticine onto the nose and mouth of the glass bust and shape it into a snout. Cut a mouth with the spatula and model the nose. Roll two long plasticine cylinders and press them onto the mouth and snout as the werewolf's lips. When you are satisfied with the shape of the snout, scrape a lined surface structure with the spatula to resemble hair.

Place the glass bust on a towel so it is stable, with the snout facing upwards. Build up a high thick wall out of ordinary clay around the modelled werewolf snout. It is essential that the wall is at least 1 cm higher than the highest point of the snout. Smooth the outer edges well, so that cracks and holes don't form on the wall. Mix water and casting plaster in a bowl; this will be poured over the snout. Mix the plaster to the same consistency as custard and pour it into the clay form around the snout. Lightly tap the table or the clay wall to release bubbles of air, but be careful not to tap too hard or the wall might leak. While the plaster is drying, it will first become very hot, then cool again. The plaster takes 2–3 hours to dry, but when it has hardened the surrounding clay can be removed. When the plaster is thoroughly dry after 3–5 hours, remove the plasticine and you are left with a negative-mould. Remove any remaining bits of plasticine and clay from the mould. Now the mould can be used for making a latex cast (see fig. 1).

Pour latex into the negative-mould, and move the mould about to distribute the latex. Pour excess latex back in the latex container (see fig. 2). Blow into the mould with a hairdryer to dry the latex: it is fully dry when it has a yellowish translucent colour. Then apply another layer of latex, and dry as

Fig. 1

Fig. 2

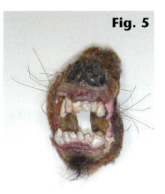

Fig. 3

It is essential that you use casting plaster for the mould, as it is stronger than modelling plaster.

Fig. 4

Fig. 5

before. Apply 4–5 layers of latex altogether. Powder the form when the final layer is dry, so the latex doesn't stick together when you remove the modelled part. Carefully loosen an edge of the latex and pull off the snout-piece (see fig. 3).

Now you can colour the snout-piece in black and brown tones with cream make-up. Paint the lips black, and dark red inside the mouth (see fig. 4). If you have made teeth, colour them a yellowish white. You can also glue on Cernit teeth.

Cut small pieces of prepared black and brown crepe hair into short pieces of less than 0.5 cm in length (see page 60). Dip one end of the crepe hair in latex and affix to the

snout-piece – put most on the sides. Push the hairs a bit closer together. Now we're going to glue on whiskers, and for these you can use the hairs of a brush. (You can also buy very realistic whiskers in hobby shops.) Dip one end in latex and put it on the side of the snout, holding each whisker in place until the latex is dry. Now your snout-piece is ready to be put on (see fig. 5).

Mounting and make-up

> **Materials:**
> Latex wolf-snout, mastix or prostick, a pair of pointed latex ears, water-based make-up (brown, black and reddish shades), eyebrow wax or a latex forehead-piece, brushes, crepe hair (black and brown), latex.

Glue the wolf-snout on the model with mastix or prostick. Apply glue to the inside of the snout around the edges and mount it over the nose and mouth of the model. Hold in place until the glue is dry (see fig. 6).

Roll a little ball out of eyebrow wax – about half the size of a pea – and press it onto the model's eyebrows in the direction the hairs grow. Spread it with your fingers until all the eyebrow hairs are flattened. Another method is to make a special forehead-piece (see page 38), and glue it onto the forehead and over the eyebrows (see fig. 7). Now paint the model's face in brownish and black colours using water-based make-up. The eyebrow area will blend in with the rest of the face due to the colouring, but make sure you get a natural transition between the snout and skin. Paint black around the eyes to make the eyes seem deeper-set (see fig. 8). Paint the rim of the lower eyelid red to give a sickly appearance. Mount pointed ears and paint these brown on the outside and black in the nooks and crannies. Using a brush and black colour, paint lines and wrinkles on the forehead, around the eyes and down the side of the cheeks.

Prepare some crepe hair (see page 60 on crepe hair), and mix the colours black and brown. Cut the locks of hair into little pieces of 1 cm and 4–5 cm respectively, and sort them in small piles according to length.

Dip the hairs in latex and affix them to the chin and up onto the cheeks. Mount the longer pieces to resemble beard-like facial hair (see fig. 9). Where the eyebrow wax covers the actual eyebrows, affix crepe hair as thick, bushy werewolf eyebrows. Glue them on with mastix, prostick or latex. You can also glue hair onto the tips of the pointed ears (see fig. 10).

If the model's hair is of a suitable colour and length, arrange it in a wild and messy hairstyle, e.g. by backcombing it. Alternatively, use a brownish-black bushy wig.

You can also use a pair of yellow special-effects cat's eyes contact lenses (see page 75 for more about contact lenses).

Also, make werewolf hands with crooked and hairy fingers (see page 47).

Fig. 6

Fig. 7

Fig. 10

Fig. 8

Fig. 9

Minotaur

The Minotaur from Greek mythology is half man, half bull. This creature was the son of King Minos' wife, and the snow-white bull that the hero Heracles had brought back from Crete. The Minotaur had the head and strength of a bull, but the body of a man.

When this monster was born, King Minos ordered him to be imprisoned in a specially built gigantic maze. As the Minotaur ate human flesh, King Minos decreed that each year, seven young men and women from Athens be sent into the labyrinth as a sacrifice to the Minotaur. The heroic prince Theseus, wished to stop this madness and volunteered to be one of the young men to be sacrificed. Prince Theseus succeeded in beating the Minotaur in battle and killed the monster.

Making the mask

Materials:
Cotton wool, latex, glass bowl, spatula, hairdryer, glass bust, ram's horn or something similar.

For making the Minotaur, a new way of making a latex mask will be demonstrated. This method is cheap, quite straightforward and involves modelling with cotton wool and latex. Pour latex into a little bowl and add small pieces of cotton wool in different sizes. After adding the cotton wool you should have a smudgy, soft mass which is easy to manipulate into the shape you want. Gradually build up a bull's head on the glass bust, but without the horns. To model the mouth, build up from two separate pieces, slowly creating the muzzle (see fig. 1). Make a ring where you want the horns: these will

end up being the thick skin surrounding the base of the horns, so make sure they are the right size. In the final stages you can add pieces of cotton wool directly to the bull's head. Using a spatula dipped in latex, smooth the contours and add finer detail (see fig. 2)

When the shaping is finished, dry thoroughly with a hairdryer. Carefully remove the mask from the glass bust – you will probably have to remove it in several parts (see fig. 3).

Fig. 1

Fig. 2

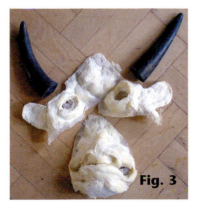
Fig. 3

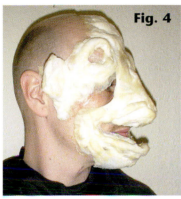
Fig. 4

latex or latex foam: for this reason, hold the mask in place against the skin until the glue is completely dry and the mask is firmly in place (see figs 4 and 5).

Now you can start colouring the mask using water-based or cream make-up. Use brownish and black colours for the base colour; paint the actual snout pink and paint dark red or black around the eyes. Choose your preferred colouring – according to which type of cow you wish to base the mask on (see fig. 6).

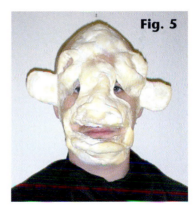
Fig. 5

Mounting the mask

Materials:
Bull's-head mask made out of cotton wool and latex, mastix or prostick, horns, brushes, water-based or cream make-up (brown, black, reddish, pink and yellowish colours), crepe hair (brown, black and yellowish colours), cotton wool, latex in a bowl, spatula.

Put the mask parts on the model one by one. Glue in place with mastix or prostick. A mask made of cotton wool and latex is a little heavier than an ordinary thin mask made of

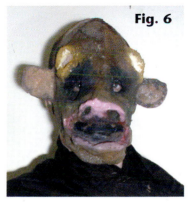
Fig. 6

Now prepare crepe hair by cutting it into little pieces of different lengths. If you like, mix different blacks and browns to get a more lively colour. Apply hair to the Minotaur's head, piece by piece. Dip one end of the lock of hair into latex, and mount it on the mask. It's a good idea to have a photograph of a cow or bull for inspiration, so you can see how the fur differs in length and thickness (see fig. 7).

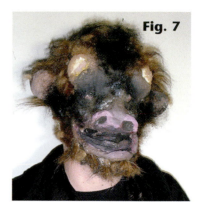

Fig. 7

The final part – mounting the heavy horns – is the most difficult. You could make latex horns, which would be much lighter, but real horns look so much better. Place one horn in the ring-shaped cotton wool–latex socket. Add more latex around and under the horn while drying with a hairdryer. Twist small strips of cotton wool dipped in latex around the base of the horn and slightly up the horn for reinforcement (don't worry if hair gets into the latex around the base of the horns). Dry at regular intervals with the hairdryer. It won't be an easy job, as the heavy horn easily sags, but with a little patience you will succeed (see fig. 8). Mount the other horn in the same way. Now colour around the base of the horn, and affix more hair to conceal the cotton wool and latex.

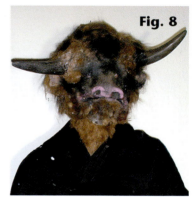

Fig. 8

For fun, you could mount a pair of artificial eyes in the eye sockets where the model would otherwise be able to see through. Then you'll have an amusing bull-man with staring eyes.

Removing the mask

Very carefully, loosen a bit of the edge and ease off the mask. If you have used mastix, dip a cotton bud in mastix-remover and rub the mastix-seam to dissolve the glue. If you have used prostick, do the same using prostick-remover. Where you have used latex alone as glue, you will simply have to peel it off carefully. It may be a little painful if you have glued on top of fine hairs, but it's really just like removing a sticky plaster. By slowly loosening the mask, you should be able to get it off in one piece.

Ever since man began to reflect on the possibility of life on other planets, our imagination has conjured up all kinds of fantastic, unearthly creatures of every shape and size. This topic has inspired writers all over the globe, and has resulted in a plethora of myths, books, comics, films, TV series and plays.

In 1947, something fell from the sky in Roswell, New Mexico. Many believe that this was a UFO, and a cult based on the existence of a certain species of alien called 'The Grays' has emerged around this incident. These beings are small and very slim, have large bald heads, and grey-brown skin. The eyes are extraordinarily big and completely dark with no iris.

It is said that these aliens come from a planet in the constellation Zeta Regue, and that they visit earth to collect gene samples of the human race. According to the story, they have degenerated on their own planet, due to the use of gene manipulation to obtain a higher intelligence. Characteristics such as emotion have been removed for rational reasons, because they were the source of wars and conflict. The result is that they have become sterile and are thus a dying species. To improve their own species, they abduct humans and subject them to bizarre genetic operations in order to create a hybrid species with a better chance of survival. A number of people, especially in the US, tell stories of being abducted in UFOs and undergoing mysterious tests and operations. Several novels, films and TV films based on this and similar themes have appeared over the years.

The best way to create an alien mask of this kind is to make a full-face mask, which you pull over your head.

Materials:

Glass bust, plasticine, spatula and utensils for modelling, latex, hairdryer, face powder or talc, scissors, gaff tape, brushes, cream or water-based make-up in all colours, ocean lacquer, disposable brush or a make-up sponge.

The following are optional: airbrush and liquid water-based make-up, Velcro.

Soften the plasticine and model large, almond-shaped eyes over the eyes of the glass bust. Apply plasticine around the nose to make the nose seem smaller, and model the mouth narrower. Scrape a couple of lines around the eyes and other surface structure details using the spatula (see fig. 1).

When the modelling is done, you are going to make a latex mould. Apply latex to the whole of the glass bust using a disposable brush, a spatula or a make-up sponge (see fig. 2). Then blow-dry the latex with cold air from a hairdryer – when it has a yellowish translucent colour, it is dry. It is essential that the mask is thick and strong, so apply 7–8 layers of latex as described above. When the final layer is completely dry, powder with face powder or talc.

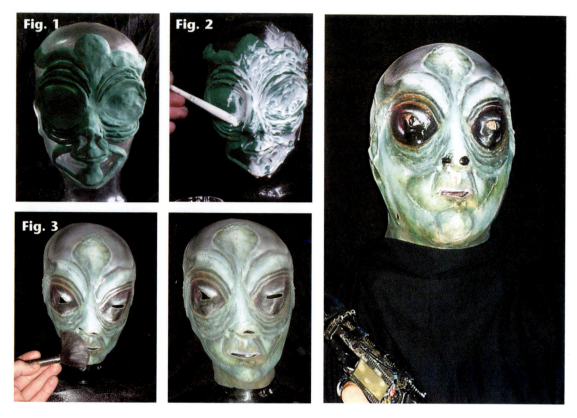

Fig. 1   Fig. 2   Fig. 3

Now you're going to remove the mask from the glass bust. However, the latex isn't elastic enough to be pulled over the chin and the back of the head, so you have to cut the mask open at the back of the neck about half way up the head. Do it carefully and make sure you get a clean cut. The two flaps at the back of the head can now be folded to one side allowing you to powder the inside of the mask. The mask should now be loose enough to be eased off the bust starting from the back of the head. Be careful not to pull the cut longer. When you've got the mask off, powder it on the inside and turn it inside out. The inside, now the outside, shows the modelled structure in more detail.

Now rinse the mask in running water. To avoid the cut getting any bigger you can put a piece of gaff tape on the inside of the mask at the end of the cut. You could also affix Velcro on the inside edges of the flap so that you can easily open and close the mask. You can glue on the Velcro with latex. Paint the mask with either water-based or cream make-up (note that if the mask is stretched or crumpled too much, water-based make-up may crumble; cream make-up, on the other hand, is more awkward to work with, and only water-based make-up can be used with an airbrush).

Paint the mask brown-grey, green-grey or blue-grey. Make sure the base colour isn't completely even, so that you have a variety of different tones. Paint hollows slightly darker and highlight raised areas using a lighter colour. Paint the eyes completely black, and add a few light streaks as reflections. If you use cream make-up, then powder the mask lightly afterwards (see fig. 3). If you use water-based make-up, simply leave it to dry. Then give the eyes 3–4 layers of ocean lacquer, allowing each layer to dry before applying the next. This will make the eyes shiny.

This kind of alien often wears tight-fitting, silver-grey suits.

Space princess

For use in science-fiction films and the like, only your imagination is the limit. However, space princesses are usually beautiful.

Materials:
Bald cap, scissors, mastix or prostick, water-based make-up (black, turquoise, green, blue, yellow), black mascara, rouge (grey), lips (dark red), brushes, airbrush, liquid water-based make-up for use with airbrush.

For this alien, a hole has been cut in a bald cap. The model's hair has then been pulled through the hole, and the bald cap mounted (see fig. 1).

Paint the face, head and neck turquoise and light-blue with water-based make-up. Also paint the ears (see fig. 2). Paint up the eyebrows in black; the sharp edges can be painted with a black eyeliner. Yellow eye shadow has been applied both under and over the eyes. Then, rouge has been laid as a darker shading and the lips have been painted with dark-red lipstick (see fig. 3). The shoulders have been painted black and turquoise using an airbrush.

Fig. 1

Fig. 2

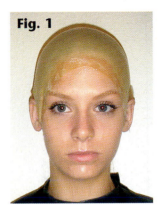

Fig. 3

Below is an explanation of the materials and products used in this book. In addition to these, other products which may come in useful are also included.

Aerosil
A latex thickener, which you add to liquid latex in a bowl.

Alginate
Fine, quick-drying casting powder which you mix with water. Alginate is commonly used to make dental impressions. It cannot be softened again once it has hardened; it is non-toxic and doesn't irritate the skin. Do not pour alginate down the sink in liquid or in dry form, as it will block the drain.

Blister gel
Stiff gel material which is very easy to work with and to remove. Has a yellowish, blister-like colour, and can be pressed onto the skin to resemble blisters or loose skin.

Blood
Artificial blood comes in many different qualities, colours and consistencies, for various kinds of use. Some kinds are very difficult to wash off clothes and wooden floors, while others clean off easily. The best-quality products look just like dried blood when dry, while the cheaper kinds look more like dry red paint. Blood often comes in two colour intensities: the lighter blood is categorised as arterial blood, i.e. blood coming from the lungs and flowing in the arteries; the darker blood is called venous blood and is on its way to the lungs to be oxidised. The latter runs in the blue veins directly under the skin. So, to get a truly realistic effect, you have to consider how deep the wound is when making up the model.

Blood capsules
Small gelatine capsules containing blood powder. Put a capsule in your mouth, break it with your teeth and you can start bleeding from the mouth suddenly, as the powder mixes with your saliva.

Blood effect for eyes
A blood product which you put into the eyes to make them look bloodshot. Drip it into the eyes using the eyedropper in the lid. The effect works for about 10–15 minutes, but can be removed right away by using eye drops. Available in red, black, blue and yellow. Once the bottle is opened, it must be used within 25 days, for hygienic reasons.

Blood paste
See *fresh scratch*.

Blood powder
A pale red powder which becomes blood-red on contact with water. The powder is almost invisible when rubbed onto the skin. 'Cut' with the blunt side of a knife dipped in water to make a 'wound'.

Bristle glue
See *Stoppelpaste*.

Cake make-up
Water-based face make-up with a high pigment content, available in a wide range of colours. Apply with a damp sponge.

Camouflage make-up
Cream-based make-up with a high pigment content. Used for concealing birth marks, beauty spots, scars, tattoos, burns and other skin blemishes you wish to hide. Fix with water-repellent face powder or fixer spray.

Casting plaster
See *plaster*.

Castogel
Silicone substance, which you soften by heating in a saucepan. Hardens again at room temperature. Suitable as an alternative casting material.

Cernit
Modelling clay available in a wide range of colours. Soften and model into the desired shape. Bake in the oven at 130°C/250°F/gas mark 1 for 15–20 minutes, then cool. Cernit is suitable for modelling artificial teeth and bones. You can coat Cernit with Fimo-lacquer after baking, if you want a glossy surface.

Clay
For modelling larger prostheses, use red or blue clay. This must be kept in an airtight bag or it will harden. When working with clay, it is a good idea to brush on a little water to keep the clay soft and easy to work with. Wrap unfinished models securely in plastic until work on them is resumed.

Clown white
Rich white cream-based face make-up, often used for Pierrot and clowns. Apply with a sponge and remove with ordinary cleansing lotion.

Coagulated blood
Very thick and dark-red blood paste for use in and around wounds which aren't completely fresh and have coagulated blood on them. Apply with a spatula.

Cold-cure acrylic
Multi-component plastic product used for casting false teeth. Consists of a strong vaporous liquid, a tooth-coloured powder and a gum-red powder. To work with this product

you must use an exhaust system and a protective facemask.

Cold foam
Multi-component latex product which expands to foam when combined. Used only for moulds with both a negative and positive mould. Must harden in open air.

Collodium
Wrinkle lacquer which you can apply to the skin to simulate old scars.

Cream make-up (greasepaint)
Rich cream colour, available in a wide range of colours. Used for facial make-up and for colouring special effects parts.

Crème stick
A concealer stick with a high pigment content, used for concealing skin blemishes and the edges of affixed latex parts. Available in a wide range of colours.

Crepe hair
Artificial hair in plaits made from acrylic or wool. Used for false beards, and on masks and bald caps. Crepe hair is available in a wide range of colours.

Dental plastic
See *cold-cure acrylic*.

Derma wax
A hard, water-repellent wax used for modelling wounds, cuts and skin deformities. Scrape the wax out of the container using a spatula and pre-soften it between your fingers. Apply the wax directly to the skin. To remove the wax, scrape it off with a spatula, and then wash the skin.

Dermplast
A product series used for skin deformities, cuts, burns and ageing. Can be combined, boiled, mixed together and made to foam.

Dermplast is non-toxic and has a pleasant smell.

Eyebrow wax
A thick wax similar to derma wax. It requires pre-softening, and you massage it onto the eyebrows in the direction of growth. Then you can paint on the wax with cream make-up, camouflage make-up or foundation in skin-colours, making it look like there are no eyebrows.

Fix blood
See *blood*.

Fixer spray
Spray lacquer that can be used on skin. Used to make tattoos, paints and special make-up last longer.

Flexible sealer
Sealing lacquer used to conceal the edges of latex masks, for instance. You can also use the sealer with Stoppelpaste to conceal eyebrows. Apply 2–3 layers using the brush supplied with the product.

Foundation
Make-up cream in skin-colours, used to even out differences in colour on the skin and as a foundation for make-up. Can be used to colour various artificial special-effects items and for toning transitions from a made-up wound to the surrounding skin.

Fresh scratch
A very thick blood paste, which looks like dried blood or flesh. Used on and around 'wounds' which are not fresh.

Friendly plastic
Hard plastic rods which become soft when dipped in boiling water. Suitable for making false teeth, bones and other plastic parts. You have to keep the water at a very hot temperature to soften this material,

which hardens again at room temperature. This product is non-toxic and available in all colours.

Gelatine (leaf gelatine)
Hardened gelatine in leaves. Used to simulate burns and for effects on the fingernails. Dissolve gelatine in boiling hot water and apply it directly to the skin when it has cooled a little.

Gelatine (powdered)
Food product made from the pulverised bones of animals. Used as a starching agent in foods and sweets. For use in special effects, mix the powder with water and bring to the boil so you get a thick porridge-like mass, then add a little glycerine. This substance is used for making burns, severe disfigurations and deformities of the skin. Little shreds of tissue paper or cotton wool can be added to the mixture to simulate sinews and bits of flesh. Apply the lukewarm mixture directly to the skin. When the gelatine is completely dry, it can be painted with cream make-up. Products and effects made using gelatine are not long-lasting as the substance is perishable. Powdered gelatine is available from butchers.

Glatzan
A liquid substance for making bald caps on a glass or plastic bust. The product gives off a lot of fumes, so you must have good ventilation during use.

Glycerine
Oily liquid, which can be used for sweat, or lymph on a burn for instance. Can also be mixed with gelatine. You can buy glycerine from most high-street chemists.

Greasepaint
Another word for cream make-up.

Hydrofix blood
Thick, water-based blood which easily washes off clothes. Comes in two colour variants: pale red and dark red.

IEW blood
'Internal, External and Washable' dark-red blood. It doesn't harm the eyes and mouth, and easily washes off clothes and wooden floors.

Kromopan
An alginate product – see *alginate*.

Laerdal blood
Thick water-based blood paste. Washes off clothes and allows heavy dilution.

Laropal
A plastic powder that melts at high temperatures. Used for casting things like artificial bottles, in special heat-resistant moulds.

Latex
Liquid rubber used for making masks, casts, wounds and artificial skin. Latex dries in contact with air and is therefore stored in an airtight container. When dry, latex becomes a yellowish translucent colour and is extremely elastic. Drying can be speeded up using a hairdryer. Latex must not be used on skin areas with cuts and grazes, or on an undiagnosed skin ailment. The latex milk is ammonia-based and gives off strong vapours: some people's skin becomes irritated and itchy on direct contact. If this happens, remove the latex immediately. Most people show no negative reaction to latex, but used directly below the eyes it may make the eyes water. Wet latex can be wiped off with a cloth or tissue paper, and dried latex can rubbed off using your fingers. Never use expensive, good-quality brushes for latex; it makes the hairs stick together. Instead, use disposable brushes, dipped in soapy water

before use; the soap prevents the liquid latex from drying. Place brushes in soapy water when not in use. Be careful not to get liquid latex on your clothes – you'll never get it off again! For this reason, always wear working clothes or an apron. Do not pour liquid or dry latex into the sink, as it will block the drain.

Latex foam
Multi-component latex compound, which expands into foam when combined. Used only for moulds with both a negative and positive mould. Hardens when baked in an oven. The moulds must always be treated with a separator before use.

Latex thickener
Thickener which you mix into latex to get a more glutinous substance. Latex thickener reduces the elasticity and durability of latex. The compound material dries much quicker and dries a whiter colour than pure latex. Latex thickener has the same effect as aerosil.

Make-up remover
Use an effective and oily make-up remover which does not irritate the skin, for instance Abschminke by Kryolan. Apply to a cloth or sponge to remove make-up.

Mastix-remover
Strong solvent for removing mastix. Apply carefully with a cotton bud. Mastix-remover is a skin irritant, so use with care.

Medicinal mastix
A very strong glue which is stronger than mastix. Remove using mastix-remover.

Milliput
A two-component plastic which can be shaped into various small parts. Dries rock-hard in 2–3 hours. Binds on wood, metal and plastic.

Modelling plaster
See *plaster*.

Naturoplast
A kind of derma wax. See *derma wax*.

Ocean lacquer
Thick gloss lacquer. Can be applied to artificial eyes, entrails and masks, to make them look glossy and more alive. On masks the dry lacquer can be used to simulate dribble or sweat.

Old Skin Plast (OSP)
Latex product applied to the skin to simulate wrinkles. After applying the product you stretch out the skin and dry with a hairdryer. When you let go of the skin again, the latex wrinkles.

Pax
A mixture of prostick and water-based paint or liquid make-up paint. This compound is well suited for painting latex parts.

Plaster of Paris
It is important that you use the right kind of plaster. Casting plaster – the type of plaster dentists use for making impressions (dental plaster) – is a very fine-grained and hard product which can be baked and is therefore well suited for making moulds. Modelling plaster is a cheaper kind of plaster which should only be used for moulds and parts that are not going to be baked or undergo rough handling. Do not pour plaster down the drain, in liquid or in dry form, as it will block the drain. Throw leftover plaster in the bin.

Plastici
Plasticine for concealing eyebrows or for modelling cuts and grazes. A kind of cross between derma wax and Softputty.

Plasticine
Often used for modelling artificial noses, ears, chins and other excrescences. Plasticine can be reused

again and again, as you can simply knead it together after use. Store in a dry place. In long-term contact with latex – in connection with latex parts, for instance – plasticine may cause the latex to swell a little and lose its shape. For this reason, do not leave latex casts on plasticine moulds for more than a day.

Powdered gelatine
See *gelatine (powdered)*.

Pro-Clean
Very skin-friendly glue remover for removing prostick.

Prostick
A very skin-friendly glue for latex parts.

Prowax
A kind of derma wax. See *derma wax*.

Rodalon
Liquid disinfectant used, in this context, for clearing brushes and make-up sponges.

Rubber make-up
Used for colouring latex parts like masks, ears, fingers, horns and other excrescences. Rubber make-up is very greasy and has a high pigment content. Rubber make-up is not the same as cream make-up: some cream make-up products are oil-based and may therefore corrode latex. However, if you don't need a long-lasting latex part, there is no reason not to use cream make-up.

Second Skin
A very dry wax product. Mix with water to get a slimy consistency, and use to simulate dissolving skin.

Separator
Thin or thick cream applied to moulds to facilitate the removal of casts. Most casting-kit series include a special separation fluid. Otherwise, you can use Vaseline.

Shellac
Lacquer of a brownish colour for coating plaster casts to make them more durable. Apply 2–3 layers.

Silicone clay
A two-component product used for making smaller moulds. Best suited for casting things which are hard and flat.

Skin flesh
Thick, fleshy gel-wax substance, which resembles cartilage. Has a light skin-colour but can easily be coloured with theatrical blood and make-up. Ideal both for open flesh wounds and severe disfigurements.

Softputty
A strong modelling wax for making wounds and skin deformities. It is strong enough to hold pieces of bone and other objects, protruding from the skin. Softputty is more difficult to smooth than derma wax.

Spezial-Teint
Cream-based make-up paint. Well suited for colouring latex parts because it is absorbed into the latex. First dip the brush in metholated spirits, then in the paint.

Spirit gum
Another word for mastix.

Stein's wax
A kind of derma wax. See *derma wax*.

Stoppelpaste
A mild glue in glue-stick form, which can be applied directly to hair and eyebrows – to affix crepe hair, for instance. You can also apply Stoppelpaste to the chin, and sprinkle little bristles over it to simulate one-day-old bristles. Washes off easily.

Theatrical blood
See *blood*.

Tooth lacquer
Lacquer applied to teeth to make it look like a tooth is missing, for instance. Dry the tooth thoroughly before applying. Can be removed by brushing the teeth, but is difficult to remove from plastic teeth. Tooth lacquer comes in black, red, nicotine yellow and white.

Tuplast
Thick substance in a tube. Squeeze onto the skin to simulate blisters. For masks, you can stretch Tuplast into 'threads' which you then mount in the mouth to create threads of slime or spit in the mouth. Tuplast can also be used for modelling scars on the skin. Press the skin together around the Tuplast, and blow-dry with cold air from a hairdryer.

Ultra Sculpt
Sculpting gel for modelling and smoothing.

Ultra Slime
Clear, slimy substance used for dribble and slime. Extremely sticky and 'threads' a lot. Sticks to anything.

Ultra Tar
Thick, black, very sticky and elastic slime-substance, which will stick to anything. Used for very severe wounds or burns where the flesh has been burned black.

UV make-up
Water-based make-up in strong neon colours. Glows under UV light. Some colours are also available as cream make-up, liquid water-based make-up and hair gel.

Water-based make-up
Water-based make-up is used for painting the face and body, artificial tattoos and other painted effects. Available in all colours; comes in liquid form in bottles, and dry form in a container.

Here is a short overview of the utensils and remedies used for creating the effects in this book.

Bristle sponge
To make up bristles or tiny haemorrhages under the skin, you use a special kind of sponge with a very coarse surface. Apply cream make-up or artificial blood to the sponge, and then dab carefully onto the skin.

Brushes
You will definitely need a selection of brushes. Use disposable or cheap brushes for latex, lacquer and materials which will ruin the brush. All brushes for make-up – powder brushes, rouge brushes, lip brushes, eye-shadow brushes, etc. – must be of a good quality. The best are marten-hair brushes, but there are many good brushes with synthetic fibres.

Wash all brushes with soap after use. When brushes have been used for making up humans, they must also be cleaned in rodalon, propyl alcohol or a similar disinfectant. If you have used them on a person with a cold sore, for instance, it may be spread to someone else via your make-up products. Furthermore, never apply products such as foundation or cream make-up to someone's face directly from the container: put a little of the product onto a palette or your hand, and work from there. This way, you avoid bacteria being transferred from brushes and sponges to your make-up products.

Ear syringe
An ear syringe, which looks like a little orange rubber ball with a nozzle, is normally used to pump water into the ear to clean it. An ear syringe can also be used for artificial blood, and the nozzle fits most rubber tubes. The syringe comes in two different sizes and is available

from most high-street chemists. If you want a continuous stream of blood, it's better to use an ordinary syringe (the type with no needle), as the ear syringe will suck the blood back in again when it re-inflates after being emptied. However, this effect can be exploited to make something move or look like it's breathing, by mounting the end of the tube under a piece of latex skin and pumping air through.

Gaff tape
A heavy-duty sticky tape which is a 'must' when you're working with film production. Comes in a grey and black. The black variant is slightly stronger than the grey.

Hairdryer
You'll need a hairdryer which can blow both cold and hot air. Some of the materials used in special effects – gelatine, for instance – must be dried with cold air, as hot air will merely melt them.

Modelling busts
Glass or plastic busts are used for modelling masks and bald caps. You can buy them transparent and in various colours. Polystyrene busts cannot be used for modelling, as neither clay nor latex will stick properly to them. If you use a plastic bust for making bald caps, you should rub the bust down with fine sandpaper to remove any irregularities which might otherwise tear the latex.

Rubber tubing
When you want blood to spurt from a wound or a cut throat, you use a length of thin rubber tubing. You can either use very thin tubing, e.g. valve tubing, which you can buy by the yard from most bicycle shops, or a

thicker kind used for aquarium pumps or intravenous lines. Mount one end in the opening of the wound, concealed beneath the clothes and held in place with gaff tape. Affix a syringe or an ear syringe filled with theatrical blood to the other end.

Spatulas for modelling
Various utensils are available for modelling with clay and other materials. These can be made out of plastic, metal or wood. For derma wax, use a flat, round spatula made of plastic or wood.

Sponges
Make-up sponges come in many different sizes and qualities. The most common are the big round ones and the smaller triangular ones. Sponges must be cleaned in the same way as brushes. If you use a sponge for working with latex, the sponge absorbs the latex and will be ruined when it has dried.

Syringes (disposable)
Disposable syringes are used for effects where you want blood to spurt out of a wound. Fill the disposable syringe (the type with no needle) with theatrical blood and affix it to the end of a length of rubber tubing. Empty the syringe to squirt out the blood. Keep a firm grip on both the syringe and the tube when you press out the blood, so the tube doesn't come loose. If necessary, use a little gaff tape. Beforehand, press the blood all the way through the tube until it's approximately 10 cm from the end of the tube and the wound. If you don't do this, it can be very difficult to get the timing right. Disposable syringes are available from most chemists in different sizes.

UK

Charles H Fox Ltd.
22 Tavistock Street
Covent Garden
London WC2E 7PY

Tel: 020 7240 3111
Web: www.charlesfox.co.uk

Screenface
Mail order:
20 & 24 Powis Terrace
Notting Hill
London W11 1JH

Tel: 020 7221 8289
Web: www.screenface.com

Screenface shop:
48 Monmouth Street
Covent Garden
London WC2 9EP

Tel: 020 7836 3955

USA

Alcone Company Inc.
Mail order:
5–49 49th Avenue
Long Island City, NY 11101

Tel: 718 361 8373
Web: www.alconeco.com

Store:
235 West 19th Street
New York, NY 10011

Kryolan Corporation
132 Ninth Street
San Francisco
CA 94103

Tel: 415 863 9684
Web: www.kryolan.com

The Makeup Shop
131 West 21st Street
New York, NY 10011

Tel: 212 807 0447
Web: www.themakeupshop.com